Goodbye Depression

Goodbye Depression

✦

Take Control of Your Life and Get Rid of Depression
A Practical Guide Based on Personal Experience

Dalia Eliav

Illustrations by Danny Kerman

iUniverse, Inc.
New York Lincoln Shanghai

Goodbye Depression
Take Control of Your Life and Get Rid of Depression
A Practical Guide Based on Personal Experience

iUniverse, Inc.

For information address:
iUniverse, Inc.
2021 Pine Lake Road, Suite 100
Lincoln, NE 68512
www.iuniverse.com

ISBN: 0-595-28469-8 (Pbk)
ISBN: 0-595-74864-3 (Cloth)

Printed in the United States of America

Contents

Introduction

The score on the tennis court was Love-40; my opponent was leading by 5-2 in the second set after winning the first one quite easily. I had just missed the first serve and was surely losing the entire match, yet I was in ecstasy. Little did it matter that many of my serves had been double faults, that most of my volleys had landed in the net and that I was exhausted after less than an hour of play. The only thing that mattered was that I was playing tennis. It was the first time that I managed to play again, really play.

A long and bitter struggle with post-menopause depression was finally showing the first signs of success. It was still far from over but right there and then, on that tennis court, I knew that I was winning.

Tennis had been a special part of my life before. Before the disease, before the collapse, before the fall, Before. At that time I could only think in terms of Before and Now. Finally, that day on the tennis court, there appeared a glimmer of After.

Before, I was a tennis addict, spending the best two to three hours of almost every day on the courts. My trophy display case, covering an entire wall in my study, was so over-crowded that I no longer bothered to bring home the new trophies I won. There was no more room for them anyway. I took part in any seniors' tournament I could get to, often competing in several age groups with players ten and even twenty years younger than me. I even competed in men's tournaments whenever the organizers would let me. And I won a lot, including national titles several years in a row.

So when depression took hold of me and shattered my life to pieces, the loss of tennis was especially painful. More than that, in

my tortured mind it became a symbol, the incarnation of all the differences between Now and Before. Several times I went, sneaked
would be a better word, with my daughter to the club during hours
when it was deserted so I would not have to meet my former friends
and partners. We would hit the balls back and forth, my daughter
careful to place the ball where it would be easiest for me to hit it
back. This typically went on for about ten minutes before I had to
stop, my body aching from the physical strain and my mind
exhausted, all energy drained out of me. Then we would head back
home, I frustrated from one more pathetic failure and my daughter
trying to soothe me and tell me it would be better the next time. But
it was a long time before it really got better and even longer until I
dared play with anybody but my daughter again.

All that is behind me now. I am Me again, no longer the wreck
that depression made of me. The struggle is over but hardly forgotten.
The disease is subdued, even if not annihilated. Depression is still
there in the background but now I have full control over it, not it
over me.

I won my battle. It was a difficult fight and did leave some scars,
but win it I did and I came out of it with flying colors. In fact, I am
convinced that in some respects I came out of this struggle better,
stronger, more confident and more in control of my life than I had
been before.

Also, I am much wiser now, having learned from the struggle with
depression how much a person can do for herself and for her life if
she has the courage and determination to take charge.

My fight for recovery would have been much easier had I known
then what I know now about the nature of depression and about
how to overcome it. The purpose of this book is to share with other
women what I wish I had known then.

Depression during menopause is not uncommon. Many women
experience it, as did I, yet for every one of us it is a new and frightening experience. The fact that so many other women suffer from

the same problem is hardly relevant and offers no consolation. Each woman has to fight the battle on her own.

I use the terms "fight" and "battle" deliberately. Depression is a disease unlike most others. You cannot rely on the world of medicine to diagnose it, treat it and hopefully cure it, while you assume the passive role of a "patient." Depression is your war, yours to win or lose. Doctors, with all their arsenal of medications and treatments, may help, but they are not going to win it for you. You must fight this disease actively and vigorously, trusting yourself first and your inner circle of family and friends second. Doctors and medicine come in third place. And, you must be anything but a "patient."

True, hindsight has 20-20 vision. But what is hindsight for me may be an insight for someone, perhaps you or a woman you care about, who now faces the same enemy I have defeated. That is why I have tried to make this the book I wish I could have read while fighting in the trenches against depression.

This very subjective account of my experiences tells the story of depression from the inside, so to speak. I do not presume to offer medical advice, nor am I qualified to do so. This book will not tell you "how to defeat depression in 10 easy steps." It will simply tell the story of my own encounter with depression from my personal perspective. It will tell about my thoughts and feelings, about what I did right and what I did wrong, together with my own conclusions and lessons learned.

Clearly, every woman is a world unto herself and every case of depression is unique for the one involved. Yet, I am sure that most, if not all of what I have learned the very hard way is true for every woman caught up in a similar situation.

One of my main conclusions is that to win this war you must understand what is happening to you and accept the fact that you suffer from depression. Then you must make the people around you, your close family and friends, realize and accept the situation. This you must achieve while suffering from severe physical agony and extreme mental distress, while every aspect of your life, of your very being, is falling apart and while your one and only concern is to get some momentary relief. Under such circumstances it is easier to understand your condition and make others understand it by learning from the experience of other people, like myself, rather than from your own.

Then you can start to fight back and, with the help of family and the right doctors, begin your way to victory. You probably will hit many pitfalls along this way, many mistakes that can be made and many wrong turns that can be taken. I know, because I made plenty of mistakes and took so many wrong turns that for a long while I was running around in circles. The penalty for each mistake is more agony and coming a step closer to despair. Learning from the mistakes and successes of others who have traveled that road before can help you steer away from mistakes and make the right decisions. If you do, I believe that your path to victory over depression will be easier and shorter. That is my hope for you.

I also hope to help educate the people close to any woman who suffers from depression, to help them understand, at least partially, what she is going through. If you suffer from almost any other disease, at least you can talk about it and people around you will understand your condition, sympathize with you and support you in every way they can. They recognize that the disease is not your fault, only your misfortune and that it is nothing to be ashamed of. Depression is different. You cannot talk openly about it because you feel ashamed and worthless. People think you are to be blamed for your problem; they do not accept the fact that depression is an illness and do not realize that it is much harder to overcome than most other illnesses. They somehow believe that your complaints and reported sufferings are the product of your imagination, that there is nothing really wrong with you. This attitude only aggravates your problem, adding frustration and strain exactly when you are least capable of handling them. It also makes it even more difficult to communicate with the people whose support you need so desperately.

Do not blame your family and friends if they adopt such attitudes. It is their ignorance of the nature of depression that should be blamed. Medical texts, either professional or popular, may help, but few people take the initiative to study medical texts of any kind to learn about what a family member, you in this case, is suffering from. It is a lot simpler and more natural to take you to a doctor. Doctors might help change the family's attitude, but it is a very rare stroke of good fortune indeed to find a doctor who is broad-minded and considerate enough to treat your disease by instructing your family and friends.

The best way to help people understand the nature of your condition and the misery you must bear, then, is probably through a story such as mine. My family was not entirely free from the "it's your fault" attitude, at least in the beginning of my ordeal. Eventually they understood, but their education took a long time. When people close to you do understand what you are really going through from the start, their support and assistance will be more forthcoming and available to you at a much earlier stage in the struggle.

Finally, I wish to impress upon you that the struggle against depression is a learning process. There is no single recipe for success; what works for one person may not work for another. Also, there is no single way out but rather a combination of several courses of action that, if followed together and in a coordinated manner, will get you out of depression. For each person there is a specific combination that is right for her and she alone can determine what that combination is. The courses of action and the tactics presented in the second part of this book are the ingredients. Each person must come up with her own recipe. You will arrive at the right combination only through a learning process. I will share my own learning process, my trials and errors that eventually culminated in my winning combination. I hope this will help you find yours.

Part A:
A Full Circle

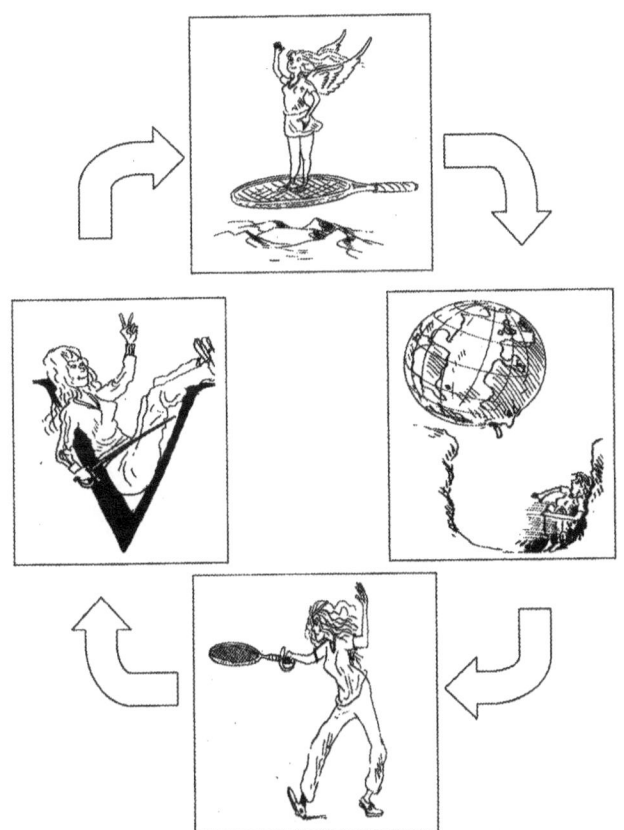

Chapter 1
The Good Days

It is about 7 p.m. Friday. I open the front door of our apartment, tennis bag on my shoulder and the sweat of nearly three hours on the court absorbed in my outfit. A tumult of noise and smells greets me at the doorstep, together with the happy tail-wagging of our dog.

Yosy, my husband, is cooking dinner. The long kitchen counters are too small for all the bowls, pots, utensils, bottles, jars, vegetables and dishes in various stages of preparation. The sink is hardly visible under a pile of dirty dishes. Several pans are on the range, the oven is on and Yosy is bustling around, appearing to be part of the chaos, not the one in control of it, while working on two or three dishes at the same time. The stereo, volume set high to be heard above the noise in the kitchen, is blaring a documentary program on history that is always on the air at this time. Every Friday when I come home, these inescapable tales of the French Revolution or some Russian Tsar follow me even into the bathroom. A strong aroma of seafood, garlic, chocolate and fresh bread fills the air. That last aroma is coming from small, snail-shaped rolls that Rotem, my youngest daughter, is baking in the oven.

The menu tonight is scallops in sauce Mornay, prawns in a white wine and garlic sauce accompanied by fresh rolls warm from the oven, followed by a three-colored chocolate mousse. Last week it was Italian, next week—who knows?

Dinner is not ready yet and I must be careful not to be anywhere near the kitchen. At this time the kitchen is off-limits for everybody except the dog, who waits under the counter for occasional morsels of food to come his way. After a quick shower I prepare to take the dog for a walk along the beach. A chunk of food persuades him to leave his lucrative position, and off we go into the silent streets of Friday evening on the short walk to the beach.

Friday in Tel Aviv is somewhat unusual. It is the first day of the weekend, and although most people are not working, all stores and businesses are open. The city is bustling with people and traffic. Stores are crowded and so are the many cafes and restaurants on the sidewalks and along the beach promenade. The pace picks up at noon and reaches a climax of jammed traffic and packed sidewalks at about 2 p.m. Then it all quiets down and a tangible shroud of tranquility settles over the city. The stores close one by one, the traffic thins out, the big noisy busses disappear from the streets along with most of the people. At about 4 p.m. the city resembles a Scandinavian town late on a summer night. It is broad daylight yet everything seems to be asleep. One might assume that the city is getting ready for the Sabbath, which sets in at sundown, but not so. The city is getting ready for the night. At about 9 p.m. the streets are full again with traffic, the restaurants are overflowing and the beach promenade, weather permitting, is packed. At midnight the activity shifts to the discotheques, nightclubs, bars and cafes. In some areas of Tel Aviv, especially along the beach, 2 a.m. Saturday is rush hour.

Back from the beach, we sit down for dinner. These dinners are a family tradition, maintained for more years than anyone cares to remember. Only my husband and I with our children. Guests, even close family, are rare. This is our time together, a special event that repeats itself every Friday. The children, all grown up now, remember these dinners as a constant part of their life since early childhood.

Our Friday dinner tradition began long before my times of trouble. We tried to maintain it even during the worst periods, and like all other aspects of my life, it is back on track now that the bad times are over.

I have come full circle. Back to where I was Before. Back to what and who I was Before. The Good Days are here again.

My day had started at another quiet hour, 5 a.m., as usual. A few minutes after waking up from a good night's sleep I was on my way to the swimming pool at the University. The city was still asleep, as if cherishing the last minutes of slumber before having to wake up to yet another noisy day. I enjoyed every moment of the short drive through the empty streets in the dim pre-dawn light.

The watchman at the gate greeted me with the usual "Hello, Dalia" and made me smile my first smile of the morning. I am one of his regular early birds. Diving into the cool water I felt the familiar sensation of its smooth, loving caress over my entire body and in my soul. The water soothed me and awakened my body. I felt my blood running, my heart beating and my body generating power. My feet pushing the edge of the pool, I started swimming in the swift, effortless style that comes from endless practice.

I started to swim competitively at the age of 17. Within a few months I had become the national swimming champion. My career as a competitive swimmer was over after a few years but I still swim every day, and I mean Swim, hard and fast and long.

For me, swimming is much more than exercise; it is an addiction. Some people pray, some do meditation, some take narcotics, some drink alcohol. I swim. I love being in water. I love being in motion in water. It makes me feel calm, comfortable and vigorous. Any ache, any stress that I may be carrying disappears the minute I feel the cool embrace of the water. The cure for fatigue is a brisk free-style swim. The remedy for tension is measured in laps.

During my long, dark period of depression, swimming was my only relief. When I could no longer drive to the pool I would walk to the beach five or six times a day and swim in the sea. Many times I went to swim in the sea at strange hours of the night and early morning, when I could not bear the pain and frustration of living. It was the only thing that made me feel alive. It was probably the thing that kept me alive.

Tennis has not been a part of my life for as long as swimming, but when I discovered it in my late twenties, it instantly became a passion and an obsession. It happened while I was pursuing my Master's degree in mathematics at the University of California in Irvine, where my husband's work took us for two years. I took a tennis course and the sport immediately pushed the Master's degree down to second priority. My life was transformed, like that of a blind person who suddenly begins to see. An eruption of a hitherto unknown natural talent for tennis, along with my explosive enthusiasm and excellent physical fitness drove my progress at an incredible pace. My coach used to say I could have been a world class player had I started at the age of ten. That opportunity, if there had ever been one, was lost, but after only two months of practice I was at the top of the Orange County tennis ladder, easily beating veteran players.

Today, my passion for Tennis is as strong as ever. When I am on the court I feel as if I am in a different world, in a sort of hard-court paradise with no worries other than my serve and forehand, with no troubles other than a partner who cheats on line calls.

I play several times a week and grasp any opportunity to play more. When I was pregnant with my youngest daughter I used to play every day, although I was already close to the age of 40. On the day she was born I played in the morning and gave birth in the evening. Of course, in the latter months of my pregnancy I could not run very well. To make up for my relative immobility, I developed an accurate and smart game that sent my opponents running all over the court while I was just standing there hitting the balls effortlessly to the edges and far corners. My fellow members at the club, many of whom I had beaten in spite of my pregnancy, figured out a way to take advantage of the situation. They would bring in players from other clubs and dare them to play against the nine-month pregnant woman, betting on me to win, which I usually did. Many cases of beer were won this way.

My efforts to get my husband and children to play have succeeded only with my son Amir and youngest daughter, Rotem. Both trained and played regularly for many years and were among the top 10 players in Israel in their age groups. Now they have abandoned tennis for martial arts. Orna, my oldest daughter tried tennis, but it was not her cup of tea. She prefers swimming, scuba diving and especially windsurfing. Yosy was a total failure at tennis. His "thing" is bicycle riding. He had been riding alone or with groups for many years before I decided that "if you cannot beat them, join them." So I got a bicycle and joined him. We have been riding together ever since, on every weekend and on vacations. For vacations we fly with our bikes to Europe, throw the bikes into the back of a rented station wagon and drive into the countryside. Once there we find a nice hotel and spend every day of the vacation on our bikes. We have done this in places such as Provence and the French Riviera, the Loire valley, the Dolomites, Toscana, Scotland, the Danube Valley and the Austrian Alps. In my opinion there is no better or more enjoyable way to experience a new place.

Recently, I have begun to run. At first it was just a whim but now I run regularly, 6 to 8 kilometers three times a week. Maybe Triathlons are next.

By profession I am a teacher. I live in Tel Aviv but teach at a high school in the middle of the Negev desert, hundreds of kilometers away. Two or three times a week I get up at 5 a.m. my usual hour, but instead of going to the pool I drive to the airport and fly to my school in the desert. I teach for about ten hours non-stop and then fly back in the evening. From the airport I drive directly to the Olympic swimming pool at the Tel-Aviv University for my daily swim.

I have always wanted to be a teacher. When I went to the university to study mathematics, right after my military service, it never crossed my mind to be a mathematician or a scientist. All I wanted to be was a teacher and now, after more than thirty years, I still greatly enjoy being one.

My first job as a teacher was in a high school in Jaffa, a low-income suburb of Tel Aviv. The first years of teaching are supposed to be difficult for the novice teacher. She is at the mercy of a bunch of unruly kids without the armor of experience, still lacking the authority and practice needed to impose discipline. Nonsense; I had a ball. It was love at first sight between the kids and me. We became good friends and Math, the bone-dry, incomprehensible anathema for all but a very few students, became fun. My classes were filled with laughter. The kids felt free and at ease, enjoying every minute. Discipline was never an issue. Yet they all worked hard, even those with no talent for mathematics, and their grades were exceptional.

The teachers went on strike during one of those first years. School was closed and the kids idle, but not my kids. They came to the small apartment we lived in at that time and we held regular Math classes with dozens of kids sitting on the floor of my living room and my baby daughter crawling around and over them.

A blast of loud music hit me when I stepped into the classroom on the last school day of my first year as a teacher. The kids had brought in a stereo system and started playing at full volume the sound track of the movie "To Sir with Love." This movie, starring Sidney Poitier, was a hit at the time. It was the story of a teacher in a rough neighborhood who manages to win the love and respect of his students. The message for me was loud and clear, especially loud. So loud that teachers and students from other classes came in to see what was going on. What they saw was like a scene from a movie; all the kids in my class dancing on the desks and me standing there, amazed and delighted.

I have taught at several schools since that first year. Short of dancing on the desks, the story is always the same. I always manage to win the respect, keen cooperation and, in most cases the affection of the kids I teach. The first thing I teach my students is self-discipline and responsibility in work habits: in writing, in thinking, in everyday conduct, in their relationship with me and among themselves, in everything they do. When that is accomplished the kids realize that I have made them become better people, capable of achieving more and of doing more. Then their respect, friendship and affection are mine. Our relationship becomes free and relaxed and they are willing to do anything I want them to, even study mathematics. I make them work hard and they do so quite willingly. I also work hard myself. Even after so many years of teaching practically the same stuff, I spend hours preparing for each class, often working long into the night.

My efforts are rewarded abundantly. The feedback from the kids is prompt and direct. My reward comes in the form of their attitude towards me, their appreciation of what I do for them, the pride and happiness of their achievements and the special sense of fellowship, of feeling good just being together with me. My reward also comes from knowing that what I give to these young people will be with them for the rest of their lives and that their lives will be better because of that. I can think of no better reward.

For me, teaching is not a profession; it is not what I do, it is what I am.

And then there is my family, my greatest, most glorious achievement.

My husband Yosy and I were high-school classmates. Just classmates, nothing more. Five or six years later I ran into him in the street. while I was walking with my parents. Small talk about the high-school days led to other things and a couple of years later we were married. About thirty years later my husband and I were walking with our oldest daughter down the street when she ran into a high-school classmate she had not seen for five or six years. A couple of years later they got married. Some things just run in the family.

Ups and downs are inevitable during nearly thirty-five years of marriage, as both people and their relationship change with the passage of time. Looking back on my marriage, the ups and downs were mere ripples, temporary perturbations that came and went without leaving a scratch. True, my marriage does change with time. It is getting better and stronger. Strong enough to hold through my long struggle with depression and to be instrumental in winning it.

Chapter 2
The Fall

I am the least likely person to suffer from depression you could possibly imagine.

I have what you might call a strong, assertive personality, always in control of myself and of everything around me. The life I lead is a flurry of many activities dominated by a rigid, efficient routine that allows me to cram into one week what most people could never achieve in a month. I am an athlete, with the strong will and self-discipline that are the essence of being an athlete. I have a warm, happy family, with three wonderful children and a loving, supportive husband. I have no health problems. I have no financial problems.

There was no reason whatsoever for me to fall into depression, but fall into it I did and the fall was long, hard and very painful.

At first, all my problems were physical, or so it seemed.

My feet started to ache when I was playing tennis. That was nothing to worry about because it had happened many times before. It must be the shoes, I thought, so I got new ones. No improvement. So I got a new set of orthopedic insoles. Again, no improvement. Then my lower back got stiff and it became difficult for me to bend to the ball or stretch up for the serve. Soon the stiffness turned into a dull and persistent ache. I applied my usual remedies of swimming, stretching exercises, massages by my husband and hot baths, but to no avail. Still, there was no doubt in my mind that the problem was entirely physical, most probably orthopedic.

At that point my tennis game was in shambles. My timing and coordination were gone and just getting to the ball, let alone hitting it properly, became an onerous task. This I still attributed to my physical problem. After all, one cannot be expected to play a good game of tennis with a stiff back and aching feet. My natural reaction, resulting from so many years of being in full control of my body, was to make a stronger effort, to work harder. Still, there was no improvement, just more frustration.

Then things got worse. My body deserted me. I was tired and my body ached most of the time, not just on the tennis court. Gone were my excellent physical fitness and my ability to indulge in sports with no apparent limit. With all energy drained from my body, even routine activities like driving or doing house chores became exhausting. Now my neck and head joined the rebellion. First, the back of my neck became stiff and every movement of my head caused a major discomfort, a concrete tension that would not go away even after some rest. Then a sensation of pressure built up in my head. Once it settled in, the pressure was always there, day and night, merciless and persistent.

The best way I could describe the pressure in my head was to say that it felt as if a noose of ropes inside my head and through the back of my neck was tightened with a brutal force, pulling and compressing everything inside. That's a poor description, I know. No matter how many times I repeated it to my husband and children, then to a long list of doctors, nobody seemed to understand what I was saying. The frustration was as painful as the sensation itself. My desperate attempts to explain my ever-present pressure to the people closest and dearest to me, then to supposedly proficient professionals, were met with blank, uncomprehending eyes. The sensation was so tangible, so concrete that I could almost feel the ropes with my hands as I massaged my temples and the back of my neck. Yet it was impossible to make anybody understand.

Restlessness, a constant feeling of tension and physical discomfort, engulfed me. I could not sleep. I could not do anything without a strong effort. I could not eat. I could hardly work. I could not live. Long walks along the beach at dawn, followed by swimming in the sea, offered only partial relief from the prolonged torture of every sleepless night. Just going through each day, trying to maintain a semblance of normal activity, was an exhausting ordeal.

And it had still not dawned on me that my problems were more than physiological. I had never been exposed to, let alone experienced, mental problems. I had no frame of reference other than the physical and had no clue that I should look for one, no clue that I would have accepted anyway. Nobody around me had ever suggested the possibility that my troubles had a mental origin; not my family, not my friends, not even my doctors (and that warrants a special discussion). To be honest, I am quite sure that even if somebody had made that suggestion I would have rejected it right away.

The sensations I had were all physical. The pressure in my head and the tension in the back of my neck were obviously physical. After a while they actually became physical because I constantly tried to alleviate the tension by deliberate and probably also non-voluntary flexing of the muscles in the back of the neck and in the shoulders, which added tense and tired muscles to my discomfort. My sense of exhaustion was so physical that I used to stop whatever I was doing to lie down and rest for a while. The frequency of these rests increased to the point where I would feel in the middle of some activity that I must rest right then, that I could not wait even for a few minutes until I got to a place where I could lie down. So, I developed a habit of stretching out anywhere I happened to be. A bench in the park, any piece of lawn or simply the floor; anything hard and flat would do.

All the while I continued to work on my body, doing endless stretching exercises and going to classes. I took any exercise class that showed even a vague promise of easing my physiological problems. I tried various methods, Feldenkreis, Yoga and Alexander to name a few, working hard at each of them until the inevitable realization that it was no use. I did put up a fight and kept looking for solutions, but I was looking in the wrong place and fighting the wrong enemy.

Then a piece of luck came my way, or so it seemed at the time. The Israeli Tennis Association gave away tickets to Wimbledon. A football fan would never give up tickets to the Super Bowl, a boxing fan would not refuse tickets to a heavyweight championship match and I was not going to give up an opportunity to go to Wimbledon. At about the same time my husband had to go on a business trip to a very unlikely combination of places: first Huntsville, Alabama; then Moscow, Russia. This was in the early 1990s, when Moscow was still an exotic place where not everyone could go. So, we decided to make the whole trip together. We would go to London first to be at Wimbledon, from London to Huntsville via Amsterdam, from Huntsville back to Amsterdam and then to Moscow.

This would not be an easy trip under any circumstances, let alone in my condition at that time. But the temptations of Wimbledon and Moscow were strong, I was reluctant to be away from my husband for more than two weeks and we both thought that a change of pace and place would take my mind off my problems. So, away we went on that crazy trip.

That was a big mistake. Wimbledon was not so bad. The tennis was fine and although the place was crowded I could easily find a piece of lawn where I could lie down for my mandatory rests. Walking around London to the usual shopping areas and tourist attractions was a different story. My history-loving husband enjoyed the historic sites and I made an effort not to spoil the visit for him, especially after he had gallantly feigned interest in the tennis matches at Wimbledon. So I walked around London, climbed the dome of St. Paul and visited the Tower, all the while carrying a heavy head, ready to burst with inner pressure on tense shoulders and repeatedly looking for places to lie down for a few minutes.

The situation did not improve on the long flight to Alabama. The business class seats might have been comfortable for others, but not for me. After an eternity of restless shifting in the seat I lied down on the floor between our seats and the row in front. It was not bad for a while but the stewardesses were all over me and made me sit back in the seat. They must have thought I was some kind of savage fresh from the jungle, for why would a civilized person pay a small fortune for a business class seat on a transatlantic flight only to lie down on the floor? When I could bear it no longer I sneaked into the economy class area, found an empty row of seats in the back and, unseen by the stewardess, lied down on the floor under the seats.

In Huntsville my husband went about his business and I was alone most of the day. I normally enjoy shopping, particularly because I have no time for it at home. A good sporting goods store usually can keep me pleasantly occupied for hours, but not this time. I had no interest in shopping or in anything else. The daily dinners with Yosy and his associates, all of whom I had known for some time, were tedious. I sat there among all those people talking and laughing, feeling as if they were in one world and I was in another. And my world was an empty, bleak place where I felt lonely and miserable. It was not just the discomfort and the pressure; there was something else. For the first time I began to suspect my problem was more than physical.

The flights from Huntsville to Moscow were even more grueling than the previous ones. Under continuous and very concrete pain from the pressure in my head, with the tension in my neck and spine unbearable after hours of sitting, I felt trapped in that aircraft. That noisy and vibrating tube was full of people who somehow did not appear to mind being there. Some even appeared to enjoy it. To me, however, something was terribly wrong with all those people, although I could not understand what it was. They were not just strangers; they were more like aliens, different beings in a different world close enough to touch but at the same time a million light years away. My husband, sitting beside me with book and drink, was one of them. I wanted to get out, right there and then, to get away from that seat, to escape the oppressive confinement of the airplane. I knew it was impossible but that did not matter. I wanted out, but out of what? Not just out of the aircraft, not just out of that mistake of a trip. It was something deeper, darker and more frightening that I wanted to get out of but did not know what it was.

During the stopover in Amsterdam Yosy suggested putting me on a plane back home, but the thought of having to face that trip alone, to take that responsibility upon myself, scared me more than going to Moscow.

One can hardly imagine two places more different than Huntsville and Moscow. Yosy had arranged a chauffeured car and personal guide to show me the city while he was occupied with his meetings. Valentina, my guide, and I became friends instantly. She showed me all the usual tourist places and also some places tourists never see. She took me to her shabby apartment of one tiny room and to the shops and restaurants where ordinary Russians went. She showed me the back yard of Moscow, not just the facade. It was very interesting to see how the Russians were living only a couple of years after the fall of Communism, especially since I am much more interested in people than in sites. I knew I should have been enjoying myself and even made deliberate efforts to enjoy this unique opportunity, but it was useless.

A sort of apathy separated me from the rest of the world. I felt like a goldfish in a glass bowl, visible to the world but not a part of it, not really in it. I had lost interest in what was happening in that world outside my bowl. All my attention, all my thoughts and feelings, became focused on the inside of my little isolated world, on my tensions, pressures and discomfort, now more intense than ever.

That was when I began to admit to myself that the origin of my problems was mental, not physiological. I guess I had known that for quite a while by that time, but the gap between knowing and accepting was bridged only during that trip. And the problem did not go away when the trip was over.

Not long after we got back, my husband had a heart attack, his second. He went through a cycle of hospitalization, tests, more tests, doctors and more doctors, until the verdict came in: bypass operation. Everything went well but it was a difficult process for him and for the rest of the family. He needed me and I made a tremendous effort, both physically and mentally, to be there for him, to accompany him to all the tests, to be with him in the hospital, to help make the necessary decisions, to take over the thousand small responsibilities of home and family. I somehow managed to do all that in spite of my condition, but the effort took a heavy toll. I sank deeper into the quicksand.

Then my son Amir joined the army. He had applied for several prestigious units and had gone off for several days of admission tests for each one of them. But the competition for admittance to those units was very intense and he was rejected time after time. He was finally admitted to a Special Forces unit, not the top-notch assignment he had hoped for but not far from that. So off he went for his three years in the military. I remember watching him go, a huge bag on his back. My "little baby" was going off to his combat unit, and I felt helpless. It was the first time that I could not help my child. He was on his own, and another piece of my life had been torn away.

Three months later, when he finished his first stage of basic training, we went to the graduation ceremony. All the parents seemed happy, except me. Even the pride and joy I showed my own son were phony. I did not feel any joy or anything else for that matter. My feelings were numb, my emotions blunt. All I felt was emptiness and darkness. And in that darkness lurked despair.

Chapter 3
In Search for the Right Doctor

My first encounter with doctors was straightforward and apparently unrelated to my problems; in fact it happened even before my problems had surfaced.

My menopause came relatively early but not unexpectedly. The changes in my body were just what I had anticipated after talking to other women. In fact, I hardly felt some of the symptoms other women complained about, which I accredited to my excellent fitness and extensive athletic activities. Like most other women, I went to see a gynecologist who gave me the usual prescription for artificial hormones. Plain routine, but my body had a different opinion. It rebelled against the hormones. The sensations associated with menopause, the very sensations that the hormones were supposed to eliminate, were intensified. The gynecologist gave me another prescription, probably a different version of the same thing because there was no improvement.

At that point I made a simple decision. Why fight with artificial medications a purely natural phenomenon? If it was my time for menopause, so be it, let nature take its course. So I stopped taking the hormones and for a while I felt fine. I automatically attributed every odd or new sensation to the menopause and to the fact that I did not take hormones, so everything was fine because there was reason and sense in it all.

Things got worse, however, when the pressure in my head and the sensations of tension and lack of energy appeared, accompanied by pain in my limbs and frequent headaches. Another round with the gynecologist led to prescriptions for the same hormones I had shunned before. Why would they work now? They did not. So it must be something else, I thought, and went for a thorough general checkup. Nothing. I was completely healthy. There was nothing wrong with me, nothing except those pressures in my head and aches in all my body that turned every routine activity into an exertion; nothing except those imaginary tightropes that pulled the inside of my head down into the back of my neck.

I also experienced a sensation I could only describe as dryness. My head felt dry as a bone, inside and out. Even my hair felt dry. That was a poor and inadequate description but I could not come up with a better one. In my thoughts and talk at that time I kept using my own terminology. Like a child who creates her own words for things and expects the adults to understand them, I had created my own terminology to describe what I felt and expected the doctors to understand. They did not. I kept talking about ropes and dryness and they kept looking at me with uncomprehending eyes and obvious impatience. It was even more frustrating to get similar reactions from my family.

With indisputable medical evidence saying I was healthy and my body screaming the opposite, I decided to see a neurologist. After all, if the body was healthy the problem must be coming from another source. The brain, or nervous system, seemed to be an obvious suspect.

The neurologist, a specialist with the highest reputation and head of the neurology department in one of the foremost hospitals, examined me thoroughly. He said he suspected something but could not confirm or deny it without further tests. So he had me hospitalized to perform those tests. After a week or so in the hospital, during which time they performed every test in their inventory, he came back with the answer. On his daily rounds, accompanied by the usual entourage of lesser doctors, he told me that his suspicions were confirmed: I had Parkinson's disease. No less. A blow to the head with a sledgehammer would have been a comfort compared to that announcement of my imminent demise. The neurologist then prescribed some medication, which he quite obviously did not expect to do any good, and released me from the hospital. He was done with me.

A young doctor lingered behind after the others had marched out of the room. When he was sure they were far enough away he said in a South American accent: "Do not believe what they say and do not take that medication. It cannot be Parkinson. It must be something else." I do not know who he was and what made him say what he said, but I did follow his advice, probably because I wanted so much to believe him. I did not take that medication and kept on looking for that something else.

But the damage of that thoughtless diagnosis was irreversible, the thoughts, fears and doubts inerasable. What if the neurologist was right after all? What if I did have that dreadful incurable disease? I came back from the hospital with a storm of thoughts raging in my mind, dreadful thoughts with a will of their own, beyond my control. It was as if one of those vicious alien beings from some science fiction story had invaded my mind and taken control of my body. The torment of those thoughts was unbearable. Endless hours of frantically pacing my living room from wall to wall brought no relief, so I went to the beach to swim. It was 3 a.m. on a windy night. The waves were high and the water cold, but I plunged in and swam for what seemed to be a very long time. I swam aimlessly in the darkness, not caring about direction or distance from the shore. The rhythmic effort of swimming and the touch of the water on my body calmed my nerves and made me feel in control again. Then I turned around towards the city lights and swam back to the shore.

So neurology was out and I was looking for something else. But why? Why should I be responsible for my own diagnosis? Without any medical knowledge and suffering under the yoke of my supposedly physiological problems and unquestionably physical pain, how was I supposed to figure out by myself what was really wrong with me? For that, as I learned over time, is really what it all amounts to. By deciding which doctor to consult you actually make an assumption as to the cause of your problem. Many doctors are like that person who loses a coin in a dark alley but searches for it under the street light in the corner. The coin is evidently not there but he only knows how to look for it where there is light. A doctor tends to look for the problem under the light of his own specialty, not necessarily where the problem really is. If you go to a gynecologist, he will try to find a gynecological cause for your problem. Take the same problem to a neurologist and he will look for the neurological cause. The trouble is that, unlike our friend from the dark alley, doctors will find the coin where they are looking for it, not where it really is. The neurologist may actually decide it is a neurological problem and another specialist will conclude that it is something else. That leaves the initial diagnosis in your own hands, whether you like it or not. It is up to you to find the right type of doctor to go to and it is you who pays the price if you make the wrong choice.

So, still convinced that my problems were physiological, and still feeling constant pain in my limbs and shoulders, I went to see a muscle specialist, a highly reputable head of a research laboratory in one of the best hospitals. Unfortunately, he saw in me only an excellent test case for his research, not a person with a pressing problem desperately in need of a solution. He stabbed my muscles with long needles connected to all sorts of machines and found nothing wrong. The muscles were fine. In fact, they were in great shape. But that did not bring me any closer to a solution.

Other doctors came and went, in quick succession. A specialist in alternative medicine who gave me long, unintelligible lectures and homeopathic drugs that made me feel worse than ever. An orthopedist who assumed my problems originated in my spine. Even a Russian healer with electrifying hands, or so he claimed. The closest I came at that point to the right type of doctor was a psychologist who worked with biofeedback, but the techniques he tried to teach me with the help of his contraptions did no good. He was trying to deal with the symptoms, not with the problem.

Bumping around, more or less at random, from doctor to doctor like a ball in a pinball machine had a very bad effect on my condition. Each doctor raised some new hope, soon to be replaced by a new disappointment. Each cycle of hope and frustration drove me closer to despair. Each doctor prescribed some treatment, some drugs that turned out to be the wrong drugs and therefore had all sorts of negative effects that caused more suffering. Worse than that, those drugs and their effects confused me, driving me around in circles and making the solution even more elusive.

My troubles were more than a year old and I still did not know that I was suffering from depression. None of the doctors had pointed me in that direction, and I simply failed to stumble on the answer by myself. Or maybe I did not want to.

The writing was on the wall. Depression, spelled in many ways: body and mind depleted of energy to the last drop, a constant sensation of deep gloom, inability to find even a morsel of joy in anything at all, a feeling of being encapsulated in a dark bubble apart from the rest of the world. All those signs and more pointed towards depression, but I was looking in every other direction.

At some point along the search I went back to the gynecologists and their inevitable hormones, driven by doubts about my earlier decision to stay away from them. Maybe that had been a rash decision? Maybe I should have given those hormones more time to gain the desired effect? Maybe the gynecologists prescribed the wrong hormones or the wrong dosage? So hormones got another chance, not by themselves but in parallel with the other medical zigzags.

A few months and a couple of gynecologists later, after that trip to Alabama and Moscow, the situation deteriorated significantly. Frustrated by my failure to find out what the problem was, confused by all those doctors and tired of the trial-and-error pursuit of the elusive demon that haunted me, I sank deeper and deeper into the darkness. Worse than that, my hope for a solution and my determination to find one were fading.

Were all these doctors joined in a conspiracy against me? Were they deliberately hiding the solution from me? Unlikely, but possible. Or was my problem so terrible that they refrained from telling me about it? Most unlikely. Doctors thrive on awful problems. Was my body so unique that it puzzled all these doctors? Probably, especially since my body did not react to all the drugs they pumped into it the way they had anticipated. If that were the case, the solution would be so much harder to find.

Or maybe it was all in my imagination and there really was no real problem to begin with. Some people around me thought so. At times this thought had even crossed my husband's mind. He did not say so, of course, but he did not have to. His thoughts were like an open book to me. But I rejected this last possibility with disgust. Of course my predicament was real, not a phantom of my imagination.

Did I not feel it, physically, tangibly, in all my aching body? Yet this possibility seemed the closest to the truth I had come to in all that time. The problem was real, all right, but it was in my mind, not in my body.

Then, in a sort of off-hand way, the truth hit me in the face like a pie in a slapstick movie. The gynecologist of the month handed me yet another prescription for some new version of useless hormones and said as an afterthought: "Why don't you see a psychiatrist?" A psychiatrist? Me? True, I was unhealthy, but not insane! But after a while it dawned on me that maybe, just maybe, he was right.

The realization that my problem was more than just physical had been creeping around in the back of my mind ever since that unfortunate trip. But it did not come out in the open. It was I who kept it in the shadows. Now, released by the doctor's remark, this idea simply made sense. After trying everything else in vain, here was a new course, a new possibility. Maybe a psychiatrist would give what none of the other doctors could, an answer to the simple question: what is wrong with me?

My first psychiatrist. There is a first time for everything. This surely will be different from all the other doctor visits. After all, he cannot send me to do more tests. Tests, God how doctors love them! Their way of saying "I do not have any idea what is wrong with you" is to say: "I want you to do more tests." It buys them time. By the time you do the tests and then make another appointment, maybe something will come up, maybe something will change. How many tests have they sent me to? It seems like hundreds and all in vain.

But psychiatrists have no tests, or do they? So what will he do? Probably he will make me lie down on a couch in a semi-dark room, sit in an arm chair where I cannot see him and mumble something every now and then to let me know he is not asleep. That is what they do in the movies. But all this is nonsense. The question is what can he do to help me? How can he get those pressures out of my head? Right now the pressure is not so bad. It was much worse in the morning. It was a good idea to go to the swimming pool just before coming here. I did only one kilometer today, but it made me feel better, as always. I must remember to tell the doctor about the swimming. Maybe it will give him a clue. After all, in the water my head feels almost as before, with almost no pressure. I should have been born a fish. No, a dolphin, I like dolphins. I told other doctors about the swimming, it is part of my doctor-speech, but they all ignored it. There is one thing that makes me feel better and the doctors think it is not relevant.

My doctor-speech, how many times have I recited it? So many that I use the same words and the same sentences, the same gestures with my hands and face to show them how much I am suffering. It is like an actor playing a part, the same in every performance. But the actor goes home after the show and I cannot.

The door opens. I go in. So this is what a psychiatrist looks like. Well, what did I expect? Just another doctor, like all those others. A desk too large for the small room, medium-messy, some books to impress the patients, no couch. There is a face behind the desk. A few years younger than me, glasses, balding, looks a little tired, no smile. A doctor.

I give him my doctor-speech, not forgetting the swimming. I look at his eyes. I always look at their eyes, searching, hoping for a flicker of understanding. How can any doctor help me without understanding my pain? No flicker, the eyes remain cold, the face unchanged. No questions either. Is it all so clear or does he think it is irrelevant? I go on with my speech. A question at last. What medications do I take? Is that all that matters? OK, I take Progesterone. He writes a prescription. Hey, doctor, don't you have anything to tell me? What is wrong with me? Can you cure me? How long do I still have to suffer?

So I ask him.

"I want to check several possibilities. Take these pills and come see me again in four weeks. Then I will see how you react to the pills and maybe I will give you other pills."

No information, but at least I have learned one thing. Now I know what psychiatrists use instead of tests. They give you pills and then other pills until something works, maybe.

By the time of my first visit to that psychiatrist, my condition had become unbearable. The pressures in my head had become so intense and the effort to maintain a more or less normal life so demanding that it was a nightmare just getting through each day. Worst of all was the frustration and the anxiety. Each cycle of new doctor, new medication and then new failure had eroded my hopes and depleted my confidence. An unknown force, irresistible and relentless, was pulling me into a dark and endless tunnel. My faith in a light at the end of that tunnel was becoming fainter, replaced by a gnawing fear that the tunnel had no end at all.

So I took the pills. There was nothing better to do anyway. To my surprise, they worked. After a couple of weeks they made me feel better. The pressure in my head became more bearable and so was that ever-present feeling of desolation. Then something happened that would reappear again and again during the next couple of years. An uncontrollable, irrational fear overpowered my mind, fear of sliding back into the quicksand I had so recently begun to crawl out of. At long last there was some release from my suffering, but instead of relief and hope it brought only fear. Fear that the improvement would be temporary and that in a short while I would be back in the grip of my tormentor, whatever it was. Although the fear was clearly illogical, it was impossible to subdue. Anxiety followed the fear and soon a new torrent of thoughts was surging out of control in my mind. A few days after I had begun to feel better, my fears materialized into reality and drove me back to the starting point.

The effect of the pills was gone, but something good did come out of that experience. It made me realize that my problem really was in my mind. The problem was still nameless, as the explicit name Depression would appear in my life quite a long time later. But that made no difference since it was only a name. What did make a difference was that at last, after bouncing from doctor to doctor and from failure to failure, I knew what kind of doctor to look for. After undergoing all those unnecessary and possibly harmful medical treatments for the wrong things, I would at last be treated for the right thing. More important, I had found the hiding place of my demon. It was holed up in my mind.

That realization was both frightening and encouraging. Frightening because mental problems were a mystery to me, alien and menacing. Encouraging because I thought that being in my mind, the problem was more within my reach. A problem in my body would be accessible only to doctors and would force me into the passive role of a patient. There would be nothing to do about it except submit to medical treatment and hope for the best. I am not my body and my body is not I, so if there is something wrong with my body there is not much I can do about it directly. But the mind is different; my mind is I and as such it is subject to my will. There must be things I can do to influence my condition actively, not passively.

Chapter 4
Under Psychiatric Care

"Take these pills and see me in a month," he said. The psychiatric equivalent of "take two aspirins and call me in the morning." That was a few weeks ago. Two weeks, three weeks, who knows? Time moves at an entirely different pace now, in step with my agony. The more I suffer, the slower it moves, letting me savor every painful moment in full. So how can I tell how long ago my visit to the psychiatrist was?

I take the pills. I took one this morning with the breakfast coffee and will take another one in the late afternoon, as soon as I get home from the beach. He told me to take three each day but starting today I will take two. There is no point in calling the doctor to ask about going down from three pills to only two. I never ask any more. I did ask the first couple of times and the answers were the same: "Take those pills as I told you to. It is too early to tell if they work. Take the pills…It is too early…Take the pills…" So what is the point in asking them? They do not know. How can they? There is no way for the doctors to know, really know and understand what I am going through and what those pills are doing to me.

Here comes that awful bell again. Time to get up and go to class. Two more hours and then I can go to the swimming pool. Thank God there still is something to look forward to. Time to get up, but I cannot move. Maybe I will sit here for one or two more minutes, slumped over the table in the corner of the teachers' lounge, head resting on folded arms, eyes shut to keep out the light. The kids will not mind.

This morning was really bad. The early morning swim helped a little but then, at school, things went from bad to worse. Four hours, four endless hours in front of those kids. Standing all the time, knowing that if I sit down it may be impossible to get up again. Teaching mathematics, striving to keep my mind focused, at least partially, on Algebra or Calculus or whatever, listening to my own words as if they are coming from the mouth of a stranger. My voice is different now, lower and hardly audible from the other side of the classroom. My speech is also different, slow and calculated; every word is an effort, so every word should count. The kids must sense that something is wrong. They keep perfectly quiet, listening intently, trying to catch every word. How I wish my doctors would listen like those kids.

I am feeling all the usual things: pressure in the head, dry head, dry mouth, eyes hurting from the light, back and neck muscles tense as in a cramp, feet and knees hurting. I am also feeling some new things. I get a little dizzy; I must make a deliberate effort to focus my eyes, otherwise everything looks blurred. And then there is the headache. It is nothing new; headache has been a faithful companion since the troubles started, but today it is worse than ever. It must come from all the Herculean efforts I must make to do the simplest things, like talk, walk or drive, let alone solve a differential equation on the board. All that is usual, but the headache today is much worse than usual, so there must be something else.

It must be the new pill. The pill is the cause of this headache and of the new dizziness and blurred eyesight. It is surely the pill. At first the new pill made no difference, then, a few days ago, I thought there was an improvement. Was it real or just my wishful imagination? Who cares? I did feel a little better. The pressure was still there but my head did not feel as dry as before and the tension was almost bearable. The day before yesterday my morning swim was enough to get me through the entire day. But the dizziness arrived yesterday and drove all my usual agonies to their usual intensity and beyond. Today came headache.

If the pill is doing that then I must stop taking it. Or maybe I am taking too much? Maybe my body cannot support the dosage he gave me? The doctors say that all their psychiatric medications "work on the brain." That is the most profound explanation they would concede to a mere patient. My brain has been worked on by so many different medications that it cannot support the normal dosage of a new one.

Today I will take only one more pill, not two. Maybe that will help. Now I really must get up somehow and go to class. Two more hours to go.

Several psychiatrists treated me after that first one, and they all failed miserably. Miserably for me, that is. I did not pick them at random from the yellow pages. Each came with warm recommendations, usually from someone he or she had treated successfully. Finding them was not easy. You cannot just say to anybody, "Hey, I have a mental problem, do you happen to know a good psychiatrist?" The enquiries must be subtler, more indirect.

I kept making those enquiries, kept searching for the right psychiatrist, or rather for the psychiatrist that would be the right one for me. The search took the form of several nearly identical cycles. The first visit, which in some cases was also the last, invariably produced a prescription and nothing else. Then came a few weeks of taking the new drug, constantly examining myself for effects and side effects. In most cases, when the effects were unfavorable or at least appeared that way to me, I would try to experiment with the dosage, again inspecting myself for the effects. A few weeks later there would be another psychiatrist.

The main problem with them all was the automatic nature of their treatment. Each of them must have diagnosed my general condition the moment he or she saw me. It was apparently written all over my face in bold letters and they were all experienced, competent psychiatrists. After their instant assessment, everything I had to say simply did not matter; it was a waste of time as far as the doctor was concerned. I was frustrated by my repetitive failure to get through to them. I thought they did not listen or did not care to understand my problem. They, on the other hand, thought that they understood perfectly, at least to the extent needed for treatment, so there was nothing more to understand.

At the root of my problem lay the common psychiatric attitude towards "cases" like me. Once the situation is diagnosed as depression, which in my case usually happened right away, there is nothing to be done about the disease itself. It is incurable, they think, and there is nothing either the doctor or the patient can do about it. Least of all the patient. A person who suffers from depression will have it for the rest of his or her life. What is left for the psychiatrist to do, according to this line of thought, is to make the situation more bearable for the patient. So they treat the symptoms, not the disease, and they do this with drugs.

There are many drugs in psychiatric inventory, although probably not as many different drugs as there are different brand names. I know because I took many of them myself. It is quite obvious that there is no way of predicting the effect that any particular drug will have on any particular patient, which logically leads to a trial and error process. The psychiatrist prescribes the drug that in his or her judgment has the best chance of bringing some relief to the patient and then waits for the results. If the results are not favorable or if there is evidence of bad side effects, it is time to try some other drug.

This description of the process, of course, represents my own personal conclusions from my own personal experience. Surely, psychiatrists may dismiss my observations as unprofessional or altogether incorrect. I will not dispute the "unprofessional" part, but I do hold my conclusions to be correct and I still bear the scars to substantiate this claim.

The snag in this process is in the feedback, or at least that is how it was in my case. The only feedback the doctors received about how the medications worked came through me. Sure, my ability to describe precisely what I felt was very limited. What they heard from me must have been confusing, not to the point, unclear. That was because I was so confused myself, so bewildered after those years of torture. But I was their only source of information, there was no other. Yet, whenever I tried, as best I could, to make a psychiatrist understand what was happening to me and how I felt, I found myself looking at a blank face. The only emotion that my words triggered in them was a slight annoyance, or maybe impatience. They were not trying to understand, only to score the performance of the drug as working or not working. Everything else was unnecessary detail.

From my point of view, this attitude was inexcusable. I refused to be regarded as a passive object, as a guinea pig that has no say in whatever is done to it. Most of all, I did not accept the assumption that I had no role in fighting my own problem. There was no doubt whatsoever in my mind that, with some guidance and support, I could do a lot to fight it very effectively. But no guidance was to be had from the parade of psychiatrists I had gone through. Obviously, I had not yet found the right one, so the search had to go on.

Soon this search spiraled into a triple trial-and-error process, like a loop within a loop within a loop. I experimented with psychiatrists, trying and discarding them in intervals of two or three months. Each psychiatrist experimented with one or more different drugs. For each drug, I eventually ended up experimenting with the dosage and deciding for myself whether to take it or not.

Thinking about it with a clear mind, this process could be nothing but destructive. One cannot change medications, psychiatric or other, like socks. Each medication leaves a trace of effects that stays with you for weeks after you stop taking it. In some cases, just ceasing to take a medication left very bad effects, almost like the effects of breaking an addiction. Add to that the effects of a new drug and the result is very confusing. All sorts of sensations accompanied each switch, and I was closely watching and scrutinizing each new sensation or even the semblance of a new sensation in the hope of finding an improvement. But how could I tell whether any new thing I felt was caused by the new drug, by stopping the old drug or maybe by some interaction between the old one and the new one? Yet my decisions to reduce or increase the dosage, usually followed by a decision to try a new psychiatrist, were based mainly on what I thought to be the effects each new drug had on me. Again, thinking about it with a clear mind today, I realize that many of those decisions were premature and quite possibly unjustified. In fact, now there is no doubt in my mind that this erratic zigzag from doctor to doctor and from drug to drug drove me deeper into the hell of depression.

I keep saying "thinking with a clear mind," but a clear mind is exactly what I could not possibly have at the time. Years of suffering and frustration had deprived me of such luxuries. Driven by anxiety, impatient to find a solution and facing my problems without any professional guidance to rely on, my decisions were impulsive, often rash. Cool, objective judgment might have led to another, less painful path, and so would luck, had I been lucky enough to find the right doctor at an earlier stage. But that is all hindsight. At that time and in those conditions, the choice was clear: keep up the search for an escape or give up and drown in depression for the rest of my life. So I kept up the search and kept on paying the price for doing so.

Chapter 5
The Bottom of the Pit

It is cold on the beach this morning although I am wearing a full warm-up suit. Yosy, my husband, walking beside me, is quite comfortable in shorts and T-shirt, as are all the early-morning joggers that pass us. But I am cold.

We walk together almost every day now, our early morning routine modified to suit my condition. Until a few weeks ago I used to drive to the swimming pool at the University every morning and he used to do his 8-kilometer walk along the beach. Now I do not drive to the pool anymore. Driving out, early in the morning, is not so bad, but coming back I have to join all the morning rush hour traffic coming into the city. I cannot stand that any more. I cannot stand the slow, bumper to bumper motion, the endless waiting at a million traffic lights, all red, the horns blowing impatiently as drivers zigzag from lane to lane trying to improve their position in the crawling snake of cars. I cannot sit there, trapped in my car, through all that mayhem, even though it takes only 20 minutes at most. The swimming pool makes me feel better but the drive to get there and back is too much for me.

Now we go to the beach together. I leave my towel and other stuff near the lifeguard's hut and we walk together for one or two kilometers, depending on how badly I feel each morning. Then I turn back, walk to where I had left my stuff, and go into the water for a swim. My husband picks up the pace to his normal speed, completes his quota of kilometers and then waits for me to come out of the water. When I do, he stands there with arms spread wide, holding the towel ready to wrap my shivering body. Then we walk back home.

After breakfast I go to work.

I wonder if anybody at school knows that I am so sick. Certainly not the teachers, although some of them surely suspect that something is very wrong. It is enough just to look at me. My face is a mask of sadness, the skin sagging in deep furrows, the corners of my mouth and my eyes drooping. My hair is so dry that it is always unkempt, no matter what I use on it. I have lost some weight and my body, my once athletic, trim, physically fit body looks haggard, its movements slow and poorly coordinated. I try to stay away from the other teachers as much as possible without being rude, to avoid the usual chitchat and gossip during the breaks, to avoid the need to pretend that everything is normal.

Normal indeed. How ambiguous can this word be? After all, everything is "normal" with me. The pain of going through every hour has become normal. The uncontrollable whirlwind of frightening thoughts is *normal. My body being in shambles is normal. Normal usually means fine, OK, but in my case it simply means the opposite.*

Work is also normal, but in a different way. It is a link to things as they should be, as they once have been. It is something to hang on to with all my will power, like one would hang on to a rope over an abyss, trying to pull oneself up to safety. But most important of all, it keeps my mind occupied with something other than itself.

Left to itself, my mind goes berserk. It is impossible to describe what goes on inside my head. Words like storm, whirlwind and typhoon are not even close. It is much stronger than I am; it simply takes over and there is nothing I can do to control it. The only thing to do is not to leave my mind to itself, not to let it take over, to keep it busy, busy, always busy, without a free moment.

Even now, when I speak to myself as if speaking to some other person, pretending to hold a conversation of sorts, I do so to occupy my mind, to hold its attention, to keep it in check. There is no telling what it will do if I let go.

Work is a harness to the mind, keeping it tied up with mathematics, kids, teachers, homework, exams, exercises and dozens of small routine things that must be done every day. When it is occupied, the mind has less leeway to go on its wild course. Sure, with the way I am now, work is very difficult. Every hour is a new ordeal. But the ordeal is more of a physical nature, a struggle against physical weakness, pain and tensions. It is torture, but torture of a kind that I can better bear than the torments of the mind. In an odd way, the deliberate and constant physical effort helps keep my mind from taking over, keeps me in control.

Work has become a refuge. No matter how incredibly difficult it is to stand in class and teach, it is much better than vacations. Teachers love vacations at least as much as their students. It is an essential part of our profession. Now I dread vacations because they give my mind a chance to throw away the harnesses I try to put on it and run free.

I must keep my mind occupied all the time, while at work, while at home, while driving and while walking on the beach, always. It is most difficult to keep it busy in the evening, when I am exhausted, but my mind is ready to run off the moment it is free to do so. Watching television or reading do not help. I just dose off, let my guard down and all of a sudden my head is filled with the thoughts I have struggled all day to keep out. So I sit at the computer, inventing and solving math problems just to keep busy, just to stay awake and in control a little while longer. Last night I sat there almost until midnight, doing unnecessary work on the computer until I could no longer keep my eyes open, and then I went to bed. Night is always the worst part of the day, because I have to be alone with my mind until morning with nothing to keep it occupied. Sleep sometimes comes to my rescue, but very rarely. Most nights I lie awake, with all the thoughts that have been restrained during the day running wild.

I am back at the lifeguard's hut, my body warmed up a little by the walk and by the rays of the early-morning sun. It is time to go into the water. It will be cold, terribly cold the first few minutes, but I know it will make me feel a little better for a short while. These days, that is all I can hope for.

A couple of years of unsuccessful psychiatric treatment had not only left my problem unsolved but had actually made it much worse. Every cycle of a new psychiatrist, a new drug and then a new disappointment drove me deeper and deeper into depression. Any attempt to describe how I really felt during those years is doomed to failure. It will only produce a muddled cocktail of inadequate words like agony, pain, torture, misery, terrible, horrible, excruciating, etc., with all their synonyms, in any number of combinations. It would take a literary talent far greater than mine to even begin to express in words my mental and physical condition at that time. But how would this hypothetical talented person do that if I were totally unable to convey to him or her what I felt? The best I can do is to describe some episodes, in the hope that at least a vague semblance of the real picture will come across through the fragments.

Today I stayed home again and did not go to work. Like a few other times during the last couple of weeks, I called in sick. Ironical, isn't it, me calling in sick? Why did I not call in sick two years ago and every day since then? But now it is different. It is the end of the second term, only ten days or so until summer vacation. Vacation is on everybody's mind, teachers and students alike. Nobody teaches and nobody studies. I also have vacation on my mind, but in a different way. Vacation fills me with fear. Fear of being alone many hours each day, at the mercy of my thoughts and agonies, with nothing to occupy my mind. The fear is so intense that I cannot muster enough mental energy to go to school. And what would I do there if I went? Chat with the other teachers about vacation plans? Watch the kids, happy about their upcoming free time, while I dread mine? So I stay home.

My daughter Rotem is still at school, probably talking excitedly about vacation with her friends. Naturally she looks forward to it, but I am afraid that this year she will not be able to enjoy it as much as she deserves to. Although I never ask her, not even by way of a hint, she spends a lot of time around me. Not necessarily with me, just around me. Her very presence, just knowing that she is nearby, that I can watch her or talk to her, is a great comfort to me and she knows it. I never tell her how much her presence helps me because I do not want to impose upon her, not even slightly. I do not have to tell her. She knows it; she feels it by herself and simply stays around, with or without some excuse. But until the end of next week she will be at school every day and I will be here, alone.

At least today I am not alone. Yosy is here with me. When I told him during our walk on the beach that I would stay home, he immediately declared that he had some papers in his briefcase that he could work on at home, so that there was no need for him to go to the office. Later I heard him call his secretary, behind a closed door, to cancel his appointments. I think he is deeply worried. Lately, in my despair, I have been telling him how I could no longer bear all this and how I wished someone would give me one pill, just one, that would put an end to it all. I hear myself saying those words quite often. They come out of my mouth, in my voice, but I am not really saying them. It is as if they are being spoken by someone else. I have never stopped to think about what this all means, but now that I do, what those words can imply is sinister. Yosy must be frightened. Although he never says a word about this, I must remember not to say those things anymore.

Anyway, we are now sitting together in a semi-dark room, he at the desk pretending to work and I on the couch pretending to read. The windows are closed to keep out any noise from the street and the shades are drawn to keep out the daylight. Being enclosed in a makeshift cocoon, isolated from the world outside, makes me feel secure, especially since I am not alone. But I know this will not last. One hour at most. Then I will become restless and irritated. What will I do then? I can feel my anxiety surge at the very thought of it. Maybe the swimming pool? But how will I get there? Driving has become very difficult for me, especially during the midday traffic. Maybe Yosy will drive me to the pool? I will ask him later; he will agree of course. When we come back from the swimming pool, Rotem will be home and she will be with me through the afternoon. So today I will be OK, more or less, until evening, but what about tomorrow?

The deterioration of my condition was slow and steady. Each day was just like the one before it, the degradation from day to day too tiny to be perceptible. But over longer periods of time, months, even weeks, the deterioration became obvious. It was noticeable mainly in things that I could no longer do. All through the bad times, I kept working and doing most of the things I had been doing before. At first it was just to preserve my usual lifestyle and my personality, my self, in spite of everything. Then it became part of the struggle, a demonstration of my will to fight back and not to give up. Keeping up things as they normally were and as they should be became an end in itself, a goal for me to achieve.

I had been holding on to "doing the usual things" as a person suspended over the edge of a cliff holds on to a rope. Nevertheless, my hands were losing their grip and the rope was slowly slipping. Slowly but consistently it became too difficult for me to do those usual things. One by one, they slipped out of my life. I gave up driving during busy hours. I gave up some mundane activities like shopping. I gave up going to the movies. Worst of all, I almost gave up tennis.

We have just arrived home, Rotem and I, from the tennis club.

We played tennis. It feels good just to repeat these words over and over in my mind, but that does not make them true. Whom am I trying to deceive? True, I was on the court, dressed in a tennis outfit and holding a racket in my hand. But that was not playing tennis. Not even close.

Rotem is an excellent tennis player. She trains hard, five times a week, and does quite well in tournaments. She could have beaten me even if I were able to play as well as I did before depression. Today she used her skill for one purpose only: to hit the balls so that it would be easiest for me to hit them back. Like an adult playing with a child who steps on the court for the first time, she did everything she could to make me feel as if I was really playing. But I am not that child and this was certainly not my first time on the court.

My tennis had been declining until a couple of months ago when I stopped playing altogether. The physical fitness, athletic ability and stamina that were my trademarks have oozed out of my body little by little, leaving it a depleted empty shell, like a deflated basketball. My mind, exhausted from all the agony, struggling against its own darker sides and desperate because it was losing the fight, could not concentrate on the game. In the beginning I could no longer play with my usual partners. They became too good for me or rather, I became too weak for them. Then it became too difficult to play at all, so finally I gave up.

What is left of my tennis now is all tied to Rotem. Five times a week I drive her to her tennis training. Driving is so tough that I often skip my daily trip to the swimming pool just to avoid it. But I have not skipped Rotem's training once yet. While waiting for her, I sometimes take my racket and some balls from the trunk of the car and practice against the wall. On Saturdays, when she has no training, we drive to the club in the late afternoon, when it is nearly deserted, and play for a while. Half an hour is the most I can last on the court, although she hits every ball straight to my racket and not too hard, so that I can hit it back almost without moving. This is all that is left of my tennis. Practicing by myself against the wall and half an hour a week of hitting easy balls like a beginner.

I look up at the large display case on the wall, at the dozens of trophies won in many years of tennis competitions, in hundreds of tournaments, from club round robins to national championships. Any sense of satisfaction today's tennis experience may have provided me disappears as I look at those trophies. The satisfaction is replaced by a deep sadness.

Chapter 6
The Enemy in my Thoughts

Stealthily, behind my back, depression had found an ally: my thoughts. They were betraying me, turning against me to join forces with my archenemy.

Somewhere along the way, with no specific reason and at no specific time, I found in my mind a new attitude that was diametrically opposed to my normal way of thinking. It was a loss of motivation and a depletion of confidence, a feeling that the whole thing was not worth it, that I myself was not worth it.

A few years had already passed since my breakdown and life around me had not stopped. My children, my husband and my friends were all going on with their lives, engaging in their usual activities. True, the life of my entire family was strongly affected by my condition, they shared my suffering to the extent they could and did their best to help. Nevertheless life went on for everybody around me. And, although I was very much a part of their lives, my part was not the same as it had been before. The stream of life was flowing around me like water around a rock and moving on, but I, like the rock stuck in the mud, was not moving along with it.

The same thing was happening at work and in every other aspect of my life. People were going about their business and doing whatever they normally did. The world did not stop; it did not even slow down to wait for me. Life all around me went on like a train on its tracks and, while I was struggling frantically to stay on board, it would roll on whether I managed to do so or not.

Before, I had always been the leader, the driving force in every group of people I was part of. Now, I have been demoted to being only someone to be taken into account and to be concerned about. I was not left at the side of the road but I was not in the driver's seat either. My self-esteem was fading and although it may be an exaggeration to say that I felt worthless, I did feel that I was worth less than before.

At the same time, the cumulative frustration of repeated failures to solve my problem chewed away at my confidence and new doubts began to crawl into my mind; doubts not only about being able to find a solution but also about whether a solution was really worth finding. Whether, if and when I found it, the solution would be worth the effort and the pain. Maybe by that time the train of life will have passed me by, already accustomed to going on without me and I will never be able to catch on and get on board again.

These were new thoughts to me, entirely alien to my character, yet they were impossible to ignore. They reduced my motivation and made things even more difficult than they had already been.

Another thought process had turned against me and it is only now, in retrospect, that I am able to understand it. This process can best be described as what engineers call a diverging feedback (or feedback with positive gain). For example, consider a simple public address system that consists of a microphone, an amplifier and a loudspeaker. If you place the microphone next to the loudspeaker and tap it lightly, you will instantly hear a very loud noise. The reason is that the weak sound of your tapping is amplified to a louder sound, which is then picked up by the microphone, amplified again to make an even louder sound and so on, until the sound is very loud indeed. The output is added to the input to make a stronger input, which results in a stronger output, which is then added to the input to make it even stronger, and so on and on.

This is what my mind did to me. It acted as an amplifier to increase the magnitude of my bad feelings and then fed the magnified bad feelings back to be amplified further and further. When suffering from the manifestations of depression, I could think only about what was hurting me at the moment, fearing that the anguish would be getting worse and worrying about my ability to bear it when it did. This invariably caused anxiety and amplified the bad feeling, only to increase the anxiety some more.

The same process unfolded with my medications. My thoughts were always locked on every new medication that the doctors tried on me, looking for effects and side effects as if through a powerful magnifying glass. Any effect of the medication, real or imagined, would be magnified out of proportion and trigger anxiety and fear of even worse effects. And the worse effects would always come, although mainly as a result of the anxiety, not of the medication. Then, when I scrutinized the medication under the magnifying glass of depression, only one conclusion was possible: the medication was bad for me, although in reality it was not the medication but my thought process that was bad.

Thoughts are not merely a perception of reality. They are reality. The pains and tortures of depression were actually caused more by what I thought and how I thought than by depression itself. It would be a long and painful time before I understood the destructive power of my thoughts and found ways to reverse the process and make my thoughts work for me instead of against me. I eventually learned how to diminish my perception of what I felt rather than amplify it, and then use that perception to reduce the anxiety rather than build it up.

Chapter 7
The Ultimate Psychiatrist

My long journey through psychiatrist-land finally brought me to Dr. Sharon, and the search ended right there. She was what I had been looking for all along.

What made her different from all the others? On the face of it, not very much. I cannot judge the level of her expertise or the depth of her medical knowledge, but those were not what made her so different from all the others. She was deputy head of a psychiatric department in one of the leading hospitals, but some of her predecessors were more senior and more experienced. She gave me pills, like all the others, and like them she did not believe that I could be fully cured. Three critical factors made all the difference. First, she regarded me as a person, someone to listen to and understand. Second, she made me an active partner in the treatment, not just a recipient of pills. And third, she was always available, always there whenever I needed her.

Fifteen minutes into our first meeting it was clear that Dr. Sharon was the one I had been looking for. Later, I knew that she was the one and much later I also understood why, but the gut feeling that "this is it" came literally at first sight.

I had reached her through an indirect recommendation. Hopeless after a long series of psychiatrists, I turned for advice to the one doctor I really trusted. He was a gynecologist, not a psychiatrist, and it was obvious that my problem was not within his field. But he was the type of doctor I was looking for among the psychiatrists, an understanding, compassionate person who treated people as people, not as patients. Unlike the psychiatrists, he listened intently to what I had to say and then called a psychiatrist he knew and asked him to see me as soon as possible.

This psychiatrist turned out to be the head of a psychiatric department in one of the hospitals near Tel Aviv. He saw us, my husband Yosy and me, in a surprisingly shabby clinic late on a Friday afternoon. He looked extremely tired and was making a noticeable effort just to stay awake. Tired as he was, he listened carefully to what I said, asked a few questions and said that in his opinion I should be in a hospital because my condition was too severe to be treated as it had been until then. This was the first time that the possibility of a psychiatric hospital had ever come up, but now that it did we saw right away the logic behind it. Clearly, I could not be left any longer to continue on the course that had brought me to such a desperate situation. Something drastic and different had to be done to pull me out. He told us to report to the hospital in the morning and see his deputy. His deputy was Dr. Sharon.

At the hospital we completed all the administrative procedures and then went to see Dr. Sharon. She was too busy to see us. We had to wait in a corridor outside her office for more than an hour. Her office was a beehive of doctors, nurses and patients, the telephone ringing frequently, the door often left open for the noise of voices, mostly more than one at a time, to come out. Several times she darted out of the office, disappeared down the corridor and then came rushing back. Nagging questions began building up in my mind. Was I going to be hospitalized in this place? For how long? And what would they do to me there?

When she finally called me in, asking my husband to remain outside, I was trembling with anxiety and about to burst from the pressures inside my head. But then everything became quiet, nobody else came in, the phone did not ring and Dr. Sharon had all the time in the world for me.

For the first few minutes she listened, very attentively, asking a short question now and then for clarification. Then her questions began to probe deeper and my answers became longer and more detailed. I soon realized what was happening. It was not a doctor interrogating a patient, nor a patient complaining to a doctor. We were having a discussion, a serious, in-depth, two-way discussion of my condition. Everything I had to say was important and she wanted to hear more and more. She wanted to know about my background: who and what I was, my work and hobbies, my family. I kept asking questions, all those questions that had been either ignored or left unanswered by so many other psychiatrists. She answered some and admitted that she did not know the answer to others, explaining that we would find the answers in due course. The information I got or did not get in that conversation was far less important than the reassurance that somehow we were in this together, that the problem was no longer mine alone, that Dr. Sharon and I were going to engage in a joint effort to solve it.

There was no need for me to be hospitalized, she said, but I was in desperate need of intensive treatment and so was to come and see her twice a week. Then she gave me her home phone number and said that I should call her anytime I felt the need to do so. She was not giving me permission to call her; she was asking me to call her.

I walked away from that first of many meetings with Dr. Sharon with a new feeling. It was not just hope. Every new psychiatrist had been a new hope, soon to be refuted. This was confidence. She was the one I had been looking for; she would help me get well.

Thus began a long and intensive treatment. During the first few months we met twice a week, then once a week. The frequency went down after a while but the treatment remained just as intensive.

The treatment followed two parallel and interconnected paths: pills and guidance.

Yes, Dr. Sharon also made me take pills, but even in this she was different from all the other psychiatrists. She explained that medication was not the entire treatment, just one aspect of it that would make the other aspects possible and more effective. She explained what the medication was going to do, what the possible effects might be and how long it would take before we could find out how well it was working. I was not just given a prescription and dismissed, left to decide for myself whether it was good or bad and to experiment with the dosage on my own. As my treatment progressed, we would discuss the effects of the medication in our meetings. She helped me distinguish between real effects and imagined effects and, when necessary, she would change the dosage. This approach calmed down my inherent suspicions about medications and my resentment of being dependent on them. It reduced the anxiety and self-scrutiny that had accompanied every new medication and that eventually led me to reject so many of them. Whenever the anxiety showed up again, whenever I had doubts about the medication and whenever I just felt bad and needed help, Dr. Sharon was only a phone call away, always ready to discuss my worries and calm me down.

The end result was stability. Dr. Sharon stopped the erratic zigzag from medication to medication that had caused me so much stress and also, most probably, considerable damage. She sometimes changed medications, but very infrequently and after long and careful considerations, in which I took an active part. She regarded medications very seriously and, as a result, eventually so did I. And, having learned to trust her medications, one source of my anxiety simply faded away.

The medications were one of the means she used to stabilize my condition, to keep my head above water. They were not meant to solve the problem, just to give me enough breathing space and staying power to allow the use of other means.

At a much later phase in my treatment, I realized that sometimes she had been using my trust in her medications to leverage the entire treatment. There were many ups and downs during the three years of regular treatment. Sometimes, maybe two or three times in the entire period, when we were losing ground and all attempts to keep my head above water were getting nowhere, she changed the medication just to start things moving again.

Discussions were the other path, or rather avenue of Dr. Sharon's treatment.

We had dozens of discussions during those three years, most of them quite long. I call them discussions, not consultations, because that is exactly what they were, two people discussing a set of issues openly and frankly. None of us forgot even for a moment that she was the doctor and I the patient, that we were not on equal footing, but we talked almost as if we were. I talked to her not as to a friend or to a member of my family, but not as to a doctor either. I was talking to a compassionate, understanding human being who was determined to do everything in her power to help me, a person with endless patience who was always available for me.

In all those discussions Dr. Sharon did not show even the slightest sign of annoyance or impatience, though most of them were repetitions of the same scene, with minor variations. She must have heard a thousand times my descriptions of how I felt, about the pressures in my head, about my fears. Every single time she listened attentively, making me feel that what I said was important, offering a comment or a bit of advice here and there. Then, together with me, she would analyze what I had said and guide me in what she wanted me to do. Her guidance came mostly in repetitions of the same theme, from different angles. There were neither earth shattering revelations in our discussions nor surprising twists in the plot. It was a slow, persistent process that moved in very small steps and often did not move at all. I cannot imagine how this process tested her patience, but from my point of view she had it in infinite supply.

Dr. Sharon was always available. Day or night, in the office or at home, I could pick up the phone and talk to her, and I often did. Whenever overburdened by my anxieties, unable to bear the pressures, in doubt about a medication or just in bad need of support, she was there, always ready to talk, always ready with words of encouragement.

Dr. Sharon's patience and availability helped me probably more than what was actually said in our discussions. This was my anchor, holding me steady in the stormy sea of my mind, keeping me from drifting around aimlessly at the mercy of the currents or from being pulled in by the vortex.

Most of our discussions were focused on one main purpose: to make me understand. She explained things over and over, not in medical terms, not even in the simplified language used so commonly to explain scientific issues to laymen. In fact, she hardly ever used the term Depression. Dr. Sharon talked mostly about thoughts and emotions, about what I felt and why I felt that way. She did not just explain as one would when trying to teach someone something new, as I would explain a mathematical theorem to my students. It was more like preaching, intended to make the listener believe, not just understand. She wanted me to believe, deeply and without any reservation, as a devout person believes in his or her religion, that everything was entirely within my control. That it was I, my mind, my personality who had created the problem and it was I who could solve it. She strove to uproot the perception that I was in the grip of something stronger than me, of a monster far more powerful than me, to make me realize that the culprit was my own mind and therefore it was just as strong or just as weak as myself. These are all big words, words that Dr. Sharon never used. Her approach was from the bottom, through the details, through the small daily things, not from the broader concepts and principles. It was not a lecture. It was more like a teacher or a parent leading a child step by step, nudging her gently back when she strays aside and repeating each step until the child gets it right.

She did teach me some mental techniques to relieve the pressures. She even tried psychoanalysis, which proved to be a blind alley. She used the medications as a lever when things were going badly. But in the final analysis, all those approaches were just the means we used to achieve the goal. And the goal was to create the conditions that would allow me to resolve the problem myself.

Dr. Sharon did not cure me. She kept me afloat, with my head barely above water, so that I would not sink deeper and drown in my depression. She made me a believer in myself and in my power to fight and win the battle. I truly believe that in doing all that, she saved my life.

Chapter 8
My Family

To stand up to depression, I needed something to stand on in the first place: a solid basis, a steady platform. My platform was a tripod, standing on three legs. Dr. Sharon provided two of them by stabilizing my condition and giving me faith in my ability to fight. The third leg was my family.

My family shared the learning process I went through, from believing that my problem was physiological and could be cured as soon as some doctor would come up with the right diagnosis, through realizing that the problem was mental to finally comprehending how severe and dangerous it was. Once that realization sank in, my family rallied behind me and gave me all the support it could.

But initially, they were one or two steps behind.

In the beginning, when I started to complain about pressures in my head and tension in the back of my neck, I know it did not get through to my older children and to my husband. I saw it in their eyes, felt it in their reactions and, much later, they told me so. Not that they did not believe me. They had no reason not to and they all took my complaints at face value, without any hesitation. The problem was that they did not understand why I was making such a fuss. OK, so I had some pressures in my head. Everybody has some headaches or similar problems every now and then. Muscular tension? So what. It must be the result of some cramps or simply over-exertion of my body from all the sports I was practicing. After all, I was not so young anymore, and my sports activities were excessive by any normal standards. My husband, after two heart attacks and a bypass operation, could not understand why I was making such a commotion about some cramps and headaches.

Later, even when my complaints became more intense and the picture they presented became more painful, and even when I was running around from doctor to doctor, my family still did not understand what was going on. Sure, they saw that I was suffering and did whatever they could to help. My husband was part of my doctor odyssey, going with me to all the consultations and sharing all the uncertainties and frustrations of that time. Nevertheless, he suspected that I was exaggerating, that I was making a mountain out of a molehill. Now, with hindsight, I can see that he was not entirely wrong. What I felt, what I kept complaining about, was essentially what my mind perceived, not what was actually the matter. My mind, my thought processes, amplified the problem and intensified the anxiety it caused, only to amplify it again, in a diverging cycle, until it ballooned to gigantic proportions. I was complaining about what my mind made of the problem, about the inflated balloon it had created and perceived, whereas my husband, looking from the outside, saw the situation objectively for what it was in real and concrete terms. From his point of view I really was exaggerating.

My family's attitudes changed only after we realized, I and everyone around me, that my problem was mental and that I was suffering from depression. From that point on, throughout the worst period of my ordeal, my family gave me its full support without any reservation.

My husband Yosy was with me throughout this period, trying his best to help find a solution to the problem. He took part in every step of my search, from doctor to doctor, from medication to medication. He shared my disappointments and, like me, was frustrated and worried. Mostly he was frustrated by seeing me suffer without being able to help and worried by my constantly deteriorating condition. On top of all that, he was frightened by my inadvertent allusions to the one pill that would end all the suffering once and for all.

Unable to help me directly, Yosy tried to help in other ways: taking those morning walks on the beach with me, coming home from work early every day so we could go for a bicycle ride in the park, staying home with me during the worst days. During the long years until we found Dr. Sharon, Yosy was the only one who listened to me and tried to understand how I felt. All those things certainly helped me to endure the hardships and get through day after day, but they could not get me any closer to the solution.

Yosy did his best, giving all the support he could, but the one thing he did not give me was encouragement. He was worried, frustrated and helpless and could not hide all that. It showed up in his behavior, in his speech and in his body language. It is in his nature. He is unable to hide what he feels behind a cheerful façade and come up with words of encouragement. Yet, many times that is just what I needed.

My older daughter, Orna, was at the end of her studies at the university when my fall began. Then she went on a long backpacking trip to South America and, after coming back, she left our home to live with her boyfriend.

My son, Amir, was in the Army, away from home during the worst three years of my ordeal. Then, as is customary among young Israelis right after they finish the military service, it was his turn to take the long backpacking trip to South America.

Orna and Amir gave me all the support and love they could, within the constraints of their normal life. That was the best they could do at the time and I expected nothing else.

The member of my family who helped me most, the light shining in the darkness of my life, was Rotem, my youngest daughter. She was always there for me, always smiling, cheerful and understanding. Being so young, she did not try to find any reason for my sickness. She simply sensed that I was suffering and was there always to calm me down, to let me hold and hug her, without asking any questions.

Rotem was ten years old when I had my breakdown. It is unbelievable that a girl so young could give me so much confidence and courage to go on living and fighting. She made me laugh even in the darkest hours of despair. She played tennis with me when I could not play with my regular partners. She was, ultimately, my only source of joy during those awful years. Just being with her calmed me down and made me feel more relaxed and more secure.

Rotem and I have a relationship of love and understanding, a friendship more profound than any mother-daughter relationship. Even when she was only ten, I could talk to her like to an adult, about everything, openly and frankly without holding anything back. She still is my best friend.

A few years after the breakdown, when I was already in the care of Dr. Sharon and fighting depression actively myself, my family had completed its learning cycle and was lined up behind me to give me full support. By this time Rotem was a teenager in high school, Orna was about to get married and Amir was at the end of his studies. Together with Yosy, they were a more mature and more efficient support team than they had been in the beginning. Their support constituted mainly of helping me come back from the cold into a normal and active life.

During my worst and darkest period, I lived in a sort of a world apart. In spite of working and doing all the "normal things" as much as my condition would allow, I was enclosed in a shell all my own, in limbo somewhere in this world but not quite part of it. Coming back into the normal world, doing all the "normal things" for the same reasons I had done them before and not as means to control my mind, taking full control of my life and interconnecting with the lives of those around me, all these were important milestones along the way to victory. My family was instrumental in achieving these milestones.

I believe that one of the most important things in life is to create a give-give situation. If you give to other people as much of yourself as you can, in love, attention, time, support and everything else that can make their lives better, eventually they will give you all that and more in return. All my life, I have had a give-give relationship with my family and in my time of need they were there to give me all the love and support they could possibly give. I could not have overcome my bad days without them.

Chapter 9
In Search of Self-Help

All along, starting right after the breakdown, I kept reading everything that seemed relevant to my condition. But, like everything else, my reading was misdirected. Bookstore shelves are loaded with thousands of self-help books dealing with hundreds of subjects related to health and self-improvement. It is up to the reader to know the right subject, which is very much like picking the right doctor. You look for a book that will help you discover what is wrong, but if you do not know what your problem is, how can you find the right book?

My starting point was Menopause. After all, since it had all started with Menopause there must have been some connection. So I read several books about that subject. They dealt with the symptoms and effects of menopause, most of which I did not experience. They dealt with diet and exercise, but surely in my case there was not much room for improvement in those areas. My diet had always been exemplary and my dosage of exercise could suffice for half a dozen people. Mostly, the books dealt with hormones, which was fine but not very helpful. Some of the books did mention mental issues, but mainly as a side effect of the other symptoms and as a result of feeling useless and superfluous, not as the cause for severe problems. There might have been some useful clues in those books but none of them made the necessary click. The solution was not there.

Next came "alternative medicine" or rather: alternatives to medicine. My search for something, anything, that would help took me on a winding path through several such alternative methods.

When my suspicions were still focused on the physical manifestations of my ailment, the tensions and the aches, I looked for exercise methods that could relieve them.

The Alexander technique promised to improve the body posture and help reduce muscular and skeletal tensions. It did not. Not for me, anyway. The so-called exercises were ridiculously simplistic and totally ineffective.

Yoga appeared to suit me better because it was more demanding, more physical. Some months of regular classes proved yoga to be quite physical, but in the wrong way. The exercises were not easy and required a significant effort, but were all very static. My body is built and trained for motion. Keeping it motionless or in very slow motion for hours, in all sorts of unnatural positions, was extremely difficult for me at that time. The physical and mental effort involved made me feel worse and were simply not worth it, but yoga did give me some good stretching exercises that have become part of my daily routine.

Transcendental Meditation was an exercise in futility. I had hoped that it would help me calm my nerves and achieve some peace of mind. I was expected to sit very calmly, purge my mind of all thoughts and calmly repeat a meaningless Mantra. Calmly indeed. I was anything but calm at that time and the storms of thought raging in my mind could hardly be "purged."

Reiki came next and for a while it appealed to me. The exotic idea of being able to direct the flow of energy through my body was attractive enough to be worth a try. The stories of miraculous effects on anything from the human body to a car battery achieved by merely placing a cupped hand suggested a possibility of a similarly miraculous solution to my problems. So I took a course, read some books and actually practiced what they taught. But no miracles happened. It would take much more than a cupped hand to solve my problem. At a much later stage I did come back to Reiki, but for a different purpose. It simply helps me relax.

When the realization that the problem was mental sank in and I finally knew where the enemy was, though not yet who and what it was, I started to read every book I could find on mental issues. At first my reading was sporadic but, in parallel with my continuous psychiatric treatment, it became focused on depression. I keep reading about it to this day.

Thinking back, I realize with some surprise that none of the psychiatrists who treated me ever mentioned depression. Even Dr. Sharon hardly ever mentioned the name of the disease she was treating me for. Yet, once I was on the right track it was not difficult at all to identify the enemy. The perfect match of the symptoms described in the books and what I felt left no room for doubt.

After reading so many books about depression, I probably know about it as much as a lay person can. But this is only background information. The main objective was and still is to learn how to fight depression, how to gain control over depression and deny it control over me. Knowledge about the nature of depression and about what it does to people is useful to the extent that it helps find practical means to use against the disease.

I did most of my reading about depression while it still had me firmly in its grip. Concentration on reading demanded a lot of what little mental energy was left in me. It took a deliberate effort to read each book, and I made that effort again and again. Reading gave me a sense of purpose and some hope, a sense of doing something active and positive to improve my life. I was putting up a fight or at least looking for weapons to fight with, not surrendering to the overwhelming force of my opponent. That in itself made me feel a bit better, slightly more alive. Then, of course, there was the hope of actually finding a solution, something that would actually work and rid me of the oppressor.

While reading every page, every sentence, I kept asking myself: "What can this do for me? How can this be used in practice?" Most books contained valuable information about depression, some elaborately, others superficially, but the most valuable information was either skimpy or buried underneath thick layers of eloquence. In quite a few cases it felt as if someone was giving me a sales pitch, marketing this or that theory, trying to convince, to justify. I needed no sales pitches. I was eager to accept any theory, any method, anxious just to be told what to do and I would do it, no questions asked. So reading meant digging, searching through the wealth of general information, for the specific technique, for the practical thing to do.

Digging through the information often took me on detours into books about autosuggestion, hypnosis and various other forms of therapy. It was all part of a search. Whenever that search turned up something of potential value, I applied it to the best of my ability. More often than not, it was a dead end, so I backed up and kept on searching. But the search did turn up a few techniques that did help. These techniques I tried to refine and improve.

My reading, search and experimentation began to bear fruit only when I found Dr. Sharon. The techniques she taught me dovetailed perfectly with those I had devised myself. Her explanations made me realize how and when to apply them and her support gave me the self-confidence needed for the techniques to become effective. Only then did it all begin to come together.

Furthermore, in order to assess whether a technique was working, I had to be able to isolate its effects from other factors. When I tried this or that technique while my condition was unstable, and what I felt one day could be entirely different from what I would feel the next day, there was no way of telling if the technique had any effect at all and, if it did, whether it was good or bad. Later, with my condition steady, it became possible to separate what was working from what was not and to refine the techniques that proved to be effective.

Chapter 10
Fighting Back

There was no specific point in time when I started to fight back. I had been fighting all along, from the very beginning of the breakdown, but up to a certain point I was losing the war. At first, believing the problem to be physiological, I was fighting the wrong enemy. Later, the wild careening from doctor to doctor made it impossible to put up a fight. The real fight could begin only when my condition became stable and I stood steadily on the platform erected for me by Dr. Sharon and by my family.

There were several weapons in my arsenal. In using the word "weapons" I do not wish to give an impression that, like an action movie hero I got up one day, opened the doors of an arsenal well-stocked with lethal weapons, armed myself to the teeth and set out to exterminate the enemy. It was not like that at all. I had been trying to use these techniques, these so-called weapons, for a long time but without success. At last, my weapons became effective.

I had never looked for a miraculous solution, for someone to snap his fingers and make me instantly well again. All I had always wanted was to be pointed in the right direction and to be given a fighting chance. At last, I had been given just that. And, armed with some preliminary techniques, with weapons that would still be shaped and forged along the way, I went to work. To work on myself, that is.

"Work on myself" is the term that I used at the time to describe to myself and to others what I was doing. This totally unprofessional term does, in my opinion, encapsulate the essence of how I got my life back.

I worked on myself as an athlete works on speed, as a musician works on technique, as a scientist works on research. It became a project. I had a clear goal and a set of means to help me achieve it. Everything I did was focused on that goal. All my physical and intellectual capacities were dedicated to working on my project.

My starting point was close to the bottom of the pit, and it was an uphill fight all the way from there. Dr. Sharon was doing all she could to put me at that starting point in a stable condition and to make me capable of fighting. From that point on she could do no more, except shout instructions and encouragement from the sidelines. It was all really up to me.

I started out very slowly, progressing in small hesitating steps, unsure of my footing and exploring the path as I went along.

I began by building up my daily routine, by doing a little more of the simple, mundane activities of everyday life. A couple of hours more per week at school, a few more laps in the swimming pool, a little more house work, a bit more time for shopping. My self-confidence grew with every step, allowing me to pick up the pace, to move in bigger strides towards a full, active life.

Practice of mental techniques took a similar course. A slow, tentative start followed by a faster pace when the exercises began to work for me. Initially, mental techniques were quite hard to get hold of, like an oily, amorphous blob of jell lying motionless in my open palm but slipping out of my grip if I tried to grasp it. Some techniques appeared simplistic, others illogical, almost ridiculous. Most techniques came with a theoretical explanation that was intended to convince the non-believers but usually raised so many doubts that it achieved quite the opposite. I soon decided to ignore both the theories and the reservations and just do it, as seriously and whole-heartedly as I would do physical exercises. When the mental techniques began to make a difference, I became a believer.

The process eventually progressed along four routes in parallel. It did not happen all at once and it would be a long time before I could see some order, some method in what I was doing. Only with a massive dose of hindsight can the process be described as an organized, clearly structured effort. Instead, it was a combination of many small efforts, often going in several directions all at once or ending up in blind alleys. There were setbacks, detours and much trial and error. The process was a mosaic, made up of many small pieces. Like viewing a painting in a museum, it is best to take a couple of steps back and see the entire picture rather than look closely at the pieces of the mosaic. And, with the entire picture in sight, the four routes come into view.

The first route was to keep very busy, to create for myself a daily routine so crammed with activity that there would be not a single idle moment.

One can view depression as a conflict within the mind between the "normal self," whatever that is, and an evil force that emerges from some dark corner of the mind and tries to take control over it all. This evil force is not a germ or a virus that invades the mind from outside. Rather, it comes from within. It exists, to some degree, in every mind, even in the most "normal" of minds, but as long as it stays in its corner there is no problem. In people like me, this force breaks out of its confinement and takes over one's entire mind and one's entire life along with it.

While still unable to confront the evil force that is depression in the open, I could at least deny it the freedom to do as it pleased by keeping my mind constantly busy.

Of course, it is important to understand that depression makes many normal, day-to-day activities extremely difficult. The easy way out is to give up, to do nothing. That's what happened to me. In the worst days I practically threw in the towel and wound up sitting in a semi-dark room, doing nothing and feeling sorry for myself. That was a big mistake. When the mind is idle like that, depression is free to rampage as it pleases. With nothing to stop or restrain it, depression assumes total control. But when the mind is busy, occupied with something, anything, depression cannot take control.

I learned that the best way to keep my mind busy was to fill every moment of my day with activity, to avoid idleness and not to allow myself to relax. Work, sports, house chores, studying, anything, and the more the better.

At some points along the way, I bit off more that I could chew. Driven to over-confidence by success in previous steps, eager to prove to myself and to others how much more I could do, I sometimes tried to do too much too fast. My punishment for this mistake would come swiftly in the form of my all too familiar symptoms of depression, so strong at times that I had to rush to Dr. Sharon for help.

I took on a second full-time job. A full-time teaching job consists of a certain number of hours per week, which can be spread out over the entire week or crammed into two or three days. I had my school in Tel-Aviv do just that and I took a second job, with the hours similarly crammed, in a regional school deep in the Negev desert. Work then completely filled up six days each week and, with exams and other stuff teachers must do at home, it filled weekends and vacations as well. I even used to work on the bumpy flights to the Negev and back.

Slowly and hesitantly at first, I also went back to tennis. In the beginning, my game was a disaster, my style in shambles and my physical fitness a faint shadow of what it had been. I lost every game; lost and played some more, lost and played until eventually my game began to improve. I never got back to my old level but at least I was playing regularly again, in the evenings after work and on Saturdays, and that was all that mattered. In addition to tennis, I also kept up my early-morning swimming routine and even started to work out in the gym a couple of times a week. In parallel with those heavy doses of work and sports I also returned to the countless normal activities of running a home and a family.

Like all things, this buildup of activity did not happen overnight. It was gradual, taken step by step over a couple of years. At every step along the way, when the load of activities became manageable, I would add something to it. Strangely enough, no matter how much I was doing, there was always room for one more thing, and then for yet another. And, the more I managed to cram into my day, the better I felt.

The second route of my project took me into the world of mental exercise. After years of reading books, taking courses and experimenting with different techniques, I formed a set of exercises that worked for me. This set became my daily mental workout, very much like any workout in the gym, or jogging or swimming. It consisted of several relaxation exercises followed by a fixed series of autosuggestion and guided-imagery exercises. I practiced that workout regularly, every day, and I still do. As with physical exercise, after awhile my mental workout became as deeply embedded in my daily routine as brushing my teeth in the morning. Something to be done as a matter of course, without any thought or planning. Also, just as with physical exercise, completing my workout each time made me feel good.

The third route was also related to mental techniques, but in a different way. I devised a set of mental exercises and mental techniques to be used as an emergency toolbox, whenever depression had the upper hand. Keeping busy and doing my mental workouts helped keep depression at bay, but not all the time or under all circumstances. There were instances every day when in spite of all my efforts the monster reared its ugly head and roared. A few moments of idleness, stress caused by any of a million possible external sources, an argument with someone, bad news on the radio, bad weather spoiling my tennis plans, something going wrong at work, any one of these triggers could be enough to build up the pressures in my head and make me feel as bad as ever before. Many times it happened with no apparent cause at all.

My mental toolbox was prepared exactly for such emergencies, stocked with guided-imagery exercises and autosuggestion phrases to bee used as needed. For example, one of the remedies for pressures in the head was a guided-imagery exercise in which I would imagine that I was wearing a very tight helmet on my head. Then I would visualize the helmet cracking and breaking up into pieces that would fly away in all directions. In cases of tension I would perform one of several relaxation exercises followed by visualizing that I was swimming against a strong current, with the water flowing through me, not around me, and my tensions being gradually washed away in the stream. I had such exercises, usually more than one, for each situation. Every time I felt bad, when my old symptoms showed up, when I felt depressed, I would perform the mental procedures in my toolbox. Refined with years of practice, these procedures had become quite effective in subduing outbursts of depression. The mere knowledge that I had at my disposal effective weapons to be used whenever needed was a big boost to my self-confidence and therefore also a weapon against depression.

The fourth route was the most elusive and abstract of all. In fact, I am not sure whether it was one of the means to fight depression or a result of that fight. It was a change in my entire outlook on life.

Before experiencing depression, I had taken many things in life for granted. Things that came easily, things that were available without an effort and could be had at any time. Big things, like health, the ability to work, the ability to indulge in sports and in anything else that gave me pleasure. Also small things, like driving my car across town, going to see a movie or shopping for shoes. All things that had always been there and would, or so I thought, continue to be there indefinitely.

Depression taught me better. So many things had changed from self-evident to impossible that my perception of life could not remain unchanged. It changed in two ways. First, I no longer took anything for granted. I recognized that everything in life that was desirable, all that was worth having, could also be lost and required an effort to keep. Knowing that and having put in such a great effort to regain so many things I had been taking for granted and lost, made everything so much more precious, so worth doing whatever it took to have and to hold.

Second, I no longer let events take whatever course they may, trusting that everything would be OK no matter what. I became more deliberate in my actions, thinking more about alternatives and consequences, planning more carefully.

This new outlook on life, be it a cause or a result of the fight against depression, gave me a sense of purpose, calm and self-reliance that certainly helped win that fight.

Chapter 11
Life After Depression

Just as there was no specific point in time when I started to fight back, there was no specific end to the fight. Nobody waved a checkered flag at the end of the race, no bell rang to end the match, no referee blew the whistle to end the game and certainly nobody raised a white flag in surrender. In fact the fight has never ended, perhaps it never will.

I am writing these words several years after the time when, by whatever criteria or by no criteria at all except for my own very subjective judgment, the battle with depression could be declared a victory.

Am I totally cured? Definitely not.

Is depression a thing of the past? Not at all. It is still present, here and now, and probably will be with me for the rest of my life.

Am I free of the symptoms of depression, like pressures and anxiety? No, not even that.

Is the treatment over? No. I do my mental workout every day and my emergency toolbox is always ready.

So why do I claim victory?

My victory did not climax in a total annihilation of depression. That I will never achieve. My victory is in pushing depression back into the dark hole in my mind where it came from and in keeping it there. My triumph is in living my life fully, in doing everything I enjoy and in enjoying everything I do. My reward is in the knowledge that depression tried to take all that away from me but I held my own and did not let it get away with it.

Depression is still there. So what? Whenever it tries to sneak out of its hole, whenever I feel the symptoms, I am ready. I have the means and the experience to push it right back and go on with my life. Most important, I know I can do it, any time and no matter what. I have no fear.

I do have something tangible to show for my victory. During the bad times I adopted the habit of wearing a green bandanna tightly tied around my head. Initially, the bandanna may have given me some illusion of relief. Later, it became a part of me, always tied around my forehead with a knot in the back, even when I went to bed. When victory came, the green bandanna disappeared inside some drawer. Some time later my husband dug it up, still tied in a loop with the knot and had a small display case built for it. Today, that green bandanna hangs on the wall of my study, next to my tennis trophies and swimming medals. It is a trophy of sorts, a symbol of the greatest victory of my life.

Part B:
How to Fight and Win

Introduction

The first part of the book is a personal account of my war with depression. The second part is a summary of what I have learned and my recommendations to people who are still seeking their own victory over depression.

Let me be very clear. These are my conclusions and my recommendations. Mine alone. I am not a professional therapist, not even an amateur. I have not studied any "case" except my own. My only qualifications come from having been there and having done it. All that I know comes from my own experience. I know what I did right and what I did wrong and I believe that I know what I should have done to make things better. I also know that what I did worked.

My recommendations in these following chapters are no substitute for professional help. In fact, one of my recommendations to you is to seek and find the right professional help. Nor are they a substitute for reading self-help books written by qualified professionals. Again, I also urge you to read such books. These chapters have one purpose and one purpose only: to share the fruits of my experience with other people in the hope that it may work for them too.

My recommendations are not independent pieces of advice, to be accepted or ignored individually. They are a complete and integrated strategy that must be applied in its entirety. This strategy does consist of several discrete tactics, each very useful in itself, but the whole is far greater than the sum of the parts.

The Winning Strategy: Take Control

A rich man once asked Hillel, one of the greatest sages in Jewish history, to teach him the entire Torah, the enormous body of Jewish law and philosophy, in one sentence (while standing on one foot, to be exact). This request only goes to show that even in the first century BC some people thought and behaved like modern day CEOs. Hillel's answer was:" Do not do to others what you do not like them to do to you, everything else is details, go and study". Believe me, it sounds better in ancient Aramaic.

If asked, like the old master, to summarize my entire doctrine regarding the battle against depression in one statement, my answer would be, "Do not expect others to solve depression for you. Take control and do it yourself. Everything else is details, go and find out." Even if this is the only advice you take from this book, writing it was well worth my effort.

Taking control does not mean facing depression all alone. On the contrary, it must be a team effort, with the doctor, the family and close friends joining forces with you in a coordinated manner. Being in control means that you must take part in the joint effort as an active member of the team, not as a patient submitting passively to the treatment of others. It means taking positive action yourself and making the other members of the team work **for** you, not work **on** you.

The easiest thing to do when suffering from depression is to become passive, to slide into a do-nothing attitude. Unfortunately, that is also the worst thing to do. In fact, it is exactly what depression "wants" you to do. The way out is in the diametrically opposite direction, the direction of action and responsibility. And, just as the do-nothing way is very easy, the way of action is very demanding.

Depression makes life very difficult. Every small, ordinary action becomes a high hurdle. Many simple things are too painful or too hard to do. The cost, in terms of effort and hardship, of performing many activities becomes so high that they are no longer worth doing. Therefore, duties like household chores and taking care of the family are left to others, sports and hobbies are neglected, work is done at the lowest level possible, if done at all, and social life fades away. Under such circumstances how is it possible to take on the responsibility of leading the fight against depression? How can one take on such a formidable task, a staggering undertaking even for a person at the peak of his or her physical and mental power?

Furthermore, depression triggers a sense of being worthless; it shatters one's self-esteem and confidence. Yet, to take charge of the campaign against depression one must trust his or her ability to succeed, and that requires a lot of confidence.

I admit that this is a contradiction. More than that, I have no solution to offer except this: A. Contradiction or not, I know it can be done because I have done it, and B. This is the best chance you have to get rid of depression, so stop worrying about ifs and buts and contradictions, just go ahead and do it.

Just go ahead and do it? This sounds like a fine slogan, but what does it really mean? It means two things basically: conviction and perseverance.

You must understand that the best way to get rid of depression, possibly the only way, is to conduct an active campaign against it and that you are the only person in the world capable of doing that. The main purpose of this book is to convince you of this truth. But understanding is not enough unless it leads to a deep conviction, an ideology accepted as self-evident. Ideology is a big word, but not too big in the particular context of fighting depression. Once you accept it totally, without any reservation, this conviction becomes the foundation for everything that you do to win.

The ideology I am talking about is this: depression is a product of your thoughts and of your mind, stimulated by external circumstances. By the same token, depression can be undone by your thoughts and by your mind, again stimulated by external circumstances that you can create for yourself. That is all.

Simple? Maybe, or maybe it is a deep truth that is only deceptively simple. I was not born with depression. I lived happily for nearly fifty years without knowing that depression existed at all. Then, something changed in the circumstances of my life, or in my way of thinking, or both, and all of a sudden I was afflicted with depression. Depression was not a disease in the normal sense of the word. Germs or viruses did not cause it, I did not inherit it in my genes and it was not a contamination. I think of it as a fault in my mind, as something gone wrong that needed fixing. What made it go wrong was a discrepancy between new circumstances like menopause or kids leaving the home and my thought processes and attitudes. My mind did not adjust to the new circumstances or simply refused to accept them and what they implied. My thought processes, forged in nearly a lifetime of having things my way, were too rigid to adapt to the new situation. Just as an old, woody and rigid bamboo breaks in a storm, while a flexible young bamboo simply bends, something snapped in my mind causing it to malfunction.

I cannot turn the clock backwards and undo the circumstances that caused the malfunction, but I can introduce changes in my life that will fix it. I can change my way of thinking to make it more flexible and adjustable. I can do now what I should have done in the first place and adapt my attitudes, my habits and my life in general to the new circumstances. True, it is much more difficult to fix a malfunction than to circumvent it in time. But it can be done, especially if one knows what she is doing and what she is going to achieve. Oddly enough, starting to fight back from the very depths of depression has its advantages because experiencing the tortures of depression produces the strongest motivation possible to fight it.

Can you fight depression and win? Yes, definitely and unquestionably Yes. This is the objective truth. Will you actually win? Yes, if you make a commitment to fight and if you have faith in your ability to win.

The decision to embark on this campaign is the inevitable outcome of being convinced that it is in your power to undo depression. Once you make that decision, the name of the game is perseverance, sticking with it no matter what.

Now starts a journey, probably a long one, from depression back to life. One does not start a long journey running at full speed. That will not get you very far. The right way is to start slowly, to feel the way, to gradually build up skill and confidence and then to pick up the pace a little bit at a time.

The journey will take you along several routes simultaneously. Each will seem to be winding in a different way, but in reality they are all parallel. You must advance on all routes at the same time, to press forward on all fronts.

One route is in your own conscious mind. It starts with learning about depression and how it does what it does to people. That will take you to an understanding of where the problems are and where they stem from in your particular case. Finally, this route will lead to a revision of your outlook on life in a practical, not merely philosophical way. The destination is not necessarily a new way of life, but rather a new attitude towards life that will allow you to live a full and enjoyable life in any way you choose, new or old.

On the next route you do not walk alone. Your family and close friends go along. It starts as a guided tour in which you are the guide. The objective is to educate them, to make them understand what is happening to you and how that affects your life and your relationships with them. Once you achieve this objective, your family and friends will join up to propel you forward along the way to improvement rather than push you aside or simply leave you behind at the side of the road.

Yet another route runs through doctors and medications. That means much more than just going to the doctor and taking pills. It is a search for the doctor that is the right one for you and then building a relationship of trust and understanding with him or her. This route also leads to establishing a balanced attitude towards the role of medicine and medications in the fight and to understanding what they can and cannot do.

Then there is the route that will take you through the world of mental exercises, thought techniques, physical exercises and other practical methods to actively control your thoughts and feelings. This is a learning process that combines experimentation with training until faith in these methods builds up. That process will lead to the development of a set of mental techniques tailored specifically for your character and mentality. These will become your most effective means to repel depression and subdue its effects.

Finally, your routine of everyday life is one of the most important and effective tools in the fight. This route will start with your current daily routine. Then you build up your routine gradually until it fills every moment of your day with activity. The goal is to keep the mind so occupied with constant action that depression will not have a chance to move in and take over.

All these routes are interdependent. Progress along one will facilitate an advance on the others. Distance gained on the medical route, for example, will speed your progress on the route of daily routine. A step forward in mental techniques is also a step or two towards rebuilding your attitude toward life, and so on. The reverse is also true. If you get stuck on one route it will slow down your movement on the others and the entire campaign may lose momentum. If you try to take only one of the routes, no matter which, without the others, you may never reach your destination.

The best way, in my opinion the only way, to succeed in the drive against depression is through a coordinated and coherent effort on all these routes. In this respect, your fight with depression is like a carriage that is too heavy for a single horse to pull. Several horses should be harnessed and they must all pull together in the same direction. This can only be achieved with one person in the driver's seat, and that person can only be you, nobody else.

That is what I mean by Take Control.

The alternative is to do nothing, to succumb to depression and let it take full control of your life. That is total defeat. Another easy way out is to go to the doctor and take the pills without doing anything else. That, in my opinion, is only marginally better than the do-nothing alternative. Medications for a person suffering from depression are like crutches for a person with a broken leg. Crutches are essential; it is very difficult to get by without them and silly even to try to do so. But crutches will not solve the problem and, unless other measures are taken to solve it, the problem will persist and most probably get worse until that person becomes totally depend-ent on those crutches indefinitely or ends up in a wheelchair. The same is true for medications. They are probably essential, it makes no sense to try and get by without them, but medications alone will not solve your problem. Relying on medications alone may be an easy way, but it is certainly not the way out. So take control and go to work.

To advance on all routes together is the first key to success. The second is to move slowly and persistently, at a steady walk, not in leaps and bounds. Many of the things you will do in this campaign will be new, so there is no reason to expect them to work perfectly the first time. It will take time and practice before they do, and until then, trying to do too much too soon will leave you disappointed and frustrated. Worse, it may discourage you from pursuing the fight. It is, therefore, best to proceed slowly and gradually, to build up skill and experience as you go along.

The third and most important key is to stick with it. There will be setbacks, there will be failures, there will be times when nothing will seem to work and the temptation to give up will be irresistible. All that is part of the campaign, not its conclusion. These hurdles are not defeat, not even the loss of one battle, they are just more hurdles to overcome, mere detours on the way to victory. Maybe depression is feeling threatened and is fighting back against you, maybe you tried to move too fast or maybe you took a wrong turn in the road. Investigate the reason for each setback. Find out what you were doing wrong, then correct it and press on.

TAKE CONTROL
SUMMARY

- Depression is a malfunction of the mind and you are the only one who can fix it. This fight is yours to win; nobody can do it for you.

- You must be in charge and you must take action. Passivity is defeat.

- There are several routes from depression back to life. Advance steadily and in small steps on all routes in parallel.

- Stick with it. Perseverance is the name of the game.

Tactic #1
Know your Enemy

It is impossible to win a campaign without good intelligence about the enemy. Any general will tell you that. The same holds true for the campaign against depression. It is essential to know what you are up against, to understand what it is and how it works. Otherwise, you will end up fighting windmills. Knowledge of the enemy will make your fight against it focused and will keep you moving in the right direction.

A monster that prowls in the dark is more menacing than one in the open, a hidden enemy ready to strike without warning is more threatening than one that is in plain view. So learning and understanding depression will reduce the fear of it. And, when dealing with depression, fear is more than an effect of the enemy. Fear is the enemy.

In my case, fear was the biggest barrier between improvement and me. Even when things took a turn for the better and I made some progress, fear would intervene to try and push me back to the starting point. For example, when a new medication managed to reduce the tensions and pressures in my head, the fear of these pressures remained; causing a buildup of anxiety, and the pressures would soon be back, stronger than before. The measures I took against those pressures became effective only when I finally understood what was causing the pressures in the first place and learned how to control my fears. That was also true for medical treatment and medications, which were ineffective as long as I was subject to those fears.

Thus, learning to know your enemy sets a positive cycle in motion: knowledge makes the actions you take against depression more effective and reduces the fear of depression. This, in turn, diminishes depression itself and makes the actions against it even more effective, reducing the fear even further, and so on and on.

So, what is this information that will help fight depression? It can be divided into two categories. First and foremost, you need to understand a few things about what depression is in general and what it is in your particular case. Second, you need to learn methods and techniques to combat depression.

I believe that to be effective, this effort to learn should be done in a systematic manner, not sporadically, and that the order should be general understanding first and methods second.

The enemy is in our own minds but that does not mean that we know it. It is always with us, making its presence felt in everything that we do or think, but that does not mean that we really understand it. If we perceive depression only through the effects it has on us, this perception will be partial and distorted. If the enemy is too close, you cannot see it properly without taking a few steps back. What you need is a more objective and complete knowledge of the enemy. To obtain that knowledge, you have to perceive depression by means other than your own sensations. You need sources of information that are detached from how depression makes you feel and from the thoughts it fills your mind with. Then, when you combine the objective information from such sources with your subjective experience, you will be able to see the picture as it really is.

Where is this objective information to be found? In books. Books are the best source of information. So read, and then read some more.

I know that I may be preaching to the choir here. After all, the fact that you are reading this book right now means that you do read about the subject. If that is the case, all I can offer is my very strong recommendation to continue to read about it, with some suggestions on how to do it in a systematic way.

The point is that to acquire the knowledge needed for an effective fight against depression you have to read many books about it. Not that the amount of information you need is so huge or that the level of this information is so profound that no single book can contain it. A single book can easily contain all the information you need, but that book does not exist. It will only exist if you write it yourself, because every one of us has to create his or her own picture of the issue by fusing information acquired from external sources, mainly books and doctors, with our own experience. To that end, you need to pick fragments of the picture from many different books and combine them into your own picture as you would in putting together a jigsaw puzzle.

There are hundreds, maybe thousands of books about depression on the shelves, not including professional literature and textbooks. The literature intended for the general public falls almost exclusively in the category of self-help books. I have not come across any books that deal with depression for information only, the way other books deal with evolution or cell biology, again excluding textbooks and the like. The fact that I have not encountered such books does not mean they do not exist. It only means that if they do exist, they are relatively few and hard to find compared to the abundance of self-help books.

There is nothing wrong with self-help books. Quite the opposite, they are very helpful, possibly the most helpful single ally you will find in the entire campaign. The trouble is that each of these books is trying to "sell" a method of self-help and to convince the reader of the benefits of that method. Therefore, each book explains depression from the biased perspective of the self-help method it advocates. That does not make the picture the reader gets incorrect, but it generally makes it incomplete and imbalanced. And, in most cases it is quite difficult to separate the general information about depression from the "sales pitch" of the method. So, the only way to get a clear and objective picture is to read many such books so that all the biases will average out.

At this stage the main objective is still to learn about depression, not yet to learn methods to use against it. Therefore, reading only those parts of each book that deal with the subject in general may make the task easier and shorter, provided of course that these parts can be distinguished from those that deal with the methods. If it is difficult to make this distinction, if the book dives deep into the details of the method it presents and does not contribute to your general understanding of depression, it may be a good idea to put it aside and try another book. At a later stage, when your reading becomes focused on methods and techniques, it will be time to return to that book.

Reading and learning is not an easy task while you are suffering from depression. A considerable amount of discipline and will power are needed to muster the concentration required for serious reading and to maintain it for any length of time. Therefore, it is advisable not to squander your scarce resources of attention, concentration and will power on random reading. It is better to be selective, first in choosing the books and then in reading them. If you know what you are looking for and a book does not provide it, do not invest your resources in that book. If only some parts of a book deal with what you are looking for, read those parts and leave the others for another time. Some books tend to cover valuable information under thick layers of pseudo-medical explanations that may be too verbose and too tedious for someone suffering from depression to follow. So, if reading a certain book requires too much of an effort, put it aside for the time being. The point is that a self-help book on depression is not a novel; there is no need to read it from cover to cover. My advice is to be selective, to find and read only the books, or only the chapters in each book, that contain what you need.

What, then, are you looking for?

Depression encompasses a wide range of mental phenomena that, although linked together by common psychological characteristics, can stem from many different causes and show up in many different ways. Judging from the different theories about the nature of depression and from the disagreements among professionals supporting this or that theory, I dare say, from my point of view as a total layman that I doubt whether anybody really knows what depression is.

How, then, can you or I "understand what depression is" just by reading a few books? We cannot, and we do not need to. This is neither an academic study nor a research project. The objective is very practical: to acquire a basic understanding that will form the ideological foundation for your entire campaign.

The entire doctrine of the fight against depression is based on an ideology that, like all ideologies, religious, political or any other, is most effective when accepted as a truth that needs no proof and is subject to no question. I have presented that ideology in the previous chapter, but that is not enough. I do not expect anybody to accept that ideology, or any other ideology for that matter, as gospel. That is why I bring it up in the context of learning and reading.

The only axioms of any kind that I am willing to accept as needing no proof are in mathematics. I will not accept anything as unquestionably true just because someone tells me so, and I do not expect anybody to accept what I believe in just because I say so. The purpose of reading and learning about depression is to form your own perception and convictions, your own ideology. I trust it will be very similar to mine, but it will not be mine. It will be totally yours and therefore something you can accept without question.

To reiterate, here is the basic ideology I am talking about: depression is a product of your thoughts and your mind, stimulated by external circumstances. By the same token, depression can be undone by your thoughts and your mind, again stimulated by external circumstances that you can create for yourself.

I am absolutely convinced, beyond any shadow of doubt, that these statements are true. This belief was the solid base for everything I did that eventually led to my victory over depression. Now that I am formulating what I did and what I have learned into a doctrine for the use of others, I could fill pages upon pages with arguments and declarations in an attempt to convince you of that truth and to convert you to my ideology. But I think it is better not to do so.

Do not take my word for it; go and convince yourself. This persuasion is the first and most important step on the way out of depression and it must be firm and decisive, not tentative. A "yeah, well, we'll see" attitude won't do. This is the foundation for everything you will do to get rid of depression and it must be solid. Any hesitation, any doubts, will make the foundation shaky and everything you try to build upon it will collapse.

Most of the books that deal with depression have a common theme that, although presented from many different perspectives, is basically the same as the statements I have put forth as my ideology. That becomes evident if you read enough books and extract the substance, the predominant concept from each book. At some point that common theme sinks in and becomes your own inherent conviction.

That is the time to shift the emphasis from understanding the nature of depression to learning how to undo it. Again, reading is the best way.

Now the name of the game is experimentation. There are several approaches and many specific methods in the literature. Most of them are based, in one way or another, on thought exercises and on what I would call for lack of a better term: attitude control. By thought exercises, I mean practices similar to physical exercise in that they should be performed routinely every day or several times a day. By attitude control, I mean methods for changing the way you think about life in general and about depression and its effects in particular. These changes of attitude should induce corresponding changes in your way of life and reshape it to help you cope with depression. What you are looking for is some combination of thought exercises and attitude control, because the two are tightly connected.

It is impossible and quite unnecessary to apply all the techniques you will find. The objective is to experiment with each technique, to try it on for size and fit as you would try on a pair of shoes in a store. If it does not fit, if you do not feel comfortable with it, discard it right away and look for something else. If it does fit, use it for a significant period of time, a few weeks at least, to see if it works.

This process of reading and experimentation will lead you eventually to a technique, or set of techniques of your own, created by adapting and combining elements from different books. I will present in later chapters the set of techniques that work for me, created in this manner over several years of reading and experimentation. These are the things that work for me and I believe that at least some of them will work for other people as well. But that is no substitute for reading and experimenting to create the set of techniques that work best for you.

I do not believe in one person handing a concrete technique to another person as if it was a recipe in a cookbook. In fact, that does not work very well for cooking either. These techniques are mental and intended to work on the mind. Although understanding of the workings of the mind is still vague, the theories of Freud and all his successors notwithstanding, there is no doubt that each mind is unique. So, what works for me does not necessarily work for the next person and vice versa.

Techniques and methods you find in books are just candidates, to be adopted only if they work for you. Even those that do work for you may need refinement or adaptation to your particular personality, lifestyle and mentality, until you are comfortable with them. Then they become your own personal techniques. The techniques I present in this book are no exception. Try them, and I hope that they become your own.

There is yet another aspect of learning about the enemy that cannot be ignored; yet I must admit to some hesitation in bringing it up. I refer to the attempt to analyze your own special case in order to dig up the causes of your depression. The reason for my hesitation on this issue is that all I can say is based only on my own experience and may not be applicable or true for others. Having said that, here is my opinion.

I found that digging into my own past, probing into my personality and my way of life in search for the origins of my depression, produced no practical benefit. Dr. Sharon, with my full support and confidence, invested a considerable amount of time and effort in searching for the sources of my problems. She did reach clear conclusions, which I accepted as true at the time and later realized that were completely off-track. Whether the causes she had identified were correct or false is beside the point. The point is that they were irrelevant. Knowing, or in my case believing to know the intrinsic combination of reasons for my depression did not put in my hand any means to use against it. The causes were either irreversible or conditions that had been part of my life for decades without producing depression, so it was impossible to undo them now that I did suffer from it. If anything, the search for these causes diverted Dr Sharon's attention and mine from the main task to sidetracks leading nowhere.

I therefore recommend that before starting psychoanalysis you ask yourself and your analyst the following questions: How will finding the origins of my depression help me to get rid of it? What will I do then that is different from what I can do now? Unless there is a clear and definite answer to these questions, think again.

On the other hand, I did find my discussions with Dr. Sharon very beneficial when we concentrated on what I was feeling at the time and on what I did or should do about it. These discussions were an important source of guidance. It would have been unrealistic, maybe even unfair, to expect the doctor to become a teacher and teach me what I needed to know. The discussions were no substitute for reading but rather complemented my reading with observations and insights that helped me understand what depression was all about in my particular case and what I could do to fight it.

One of the attributes of what I call "The Right Doctor" is his or her willingness and ability to provide guidance. The doctor should be a source of information, although without turning the treatment into a tutorial. He or she can answer questions, provide some basic information to get you started and point out books to read. More important, the doctor should be able to keep you from straying off track in your self-education process. Then, when you get to the phase of experimentation with various techniques, the doctor should monitor what you are doing and provide guidance when necessary.

KNOW YOUR ENEMY
SUMMARY

- You must learn about depression in order to fight it effectively.

- Reading is the best way to learn. Read many books to build a complete and balanced picture.

- Learning should convince you beyond doubt that what you do and how you think can undo depression.

- When convinced, concentrate your learning on methods to use against depression.

- Experiment with many methods to find the ones that work for you.

Tactic #2
Educate your Family

What did I know about depression before I actually got it? Nothing at all. Even after I had depression, was I able to understand what it was? I was not, at least not before suffering from it for years and investing a considerable amount of time and effort to learn about it. People who are fortunate enough not to suffer from depression cannot be expected to understand what it is or even accept its existence when exposed to depression in others. That was true for my own family, and I have no doubt that it is almost universally true for the families and friends of other people who suffer from depression.

Those fortunate people who are in the dark about depression often carry attitudes of low tolerance for it. It seems obvious to them that there is nothing really wrong with you, that all the aches and pressures you complain about are imaginary, that you are making a big fuss about nothing and that all you have to do is get a hold of yourself and simply pull yourself together. Looking back from where I am now, I admit that these derogatory perceptions were essentially correct. The aches and pressures really were imaginary in the sense that they were the products of my mind and, indeed, all I had to do was to pull myself together. In fact, all I actually did in those years of struggle was to pull myself together. But that is not what those people, in their ignorance, had meant.

The point here is that true and constructive support from the family and close friends is of paramount importance. Sympathy and commiseration are not enough. Your family must become an active member of your team; it must play a vigorous part in your efforts. Ideally, your family will be actively involved in everything that you do: forming your ideology about depression, forging your decision to fight it and persevering all the way to success. In fact, other than your own determination, family support is the most important factor in perseverance. Only family members are capable of pushing you ahead when your determination falters in the face of hardships. Only they can help you make the right decisions when temptations of easy ways out are hard to resist.

It is in your vital interest to harness your family to the effort in a full and active way, and they are most probably more than eager to join in. But there is one obstacle on the way from helpless compassion to full and active support: Ignorance.

Your family must go through a learning process similar to your own. They must learn about depression to be able to understand what you are going through and what you are doing, so that they can become part of it. In a way, it is more difficult to understand depression from the outside than from the inside. Words, written or spoken, are not powerful enough to convey the real essence of depression to people who do not experience it personally. For such people depression goes against the grain, contrary to what they know and perceive in their own minds.

So it is your job to educate your family and friends, to make them learn and understand. Do not trust them to do it without your guidance and, above all, do not assume that they understand what you tell them about how you feel.

I am blessed with a loving and supporting family that will do absolutely anything to help me. But I failed to educate them properly about depression and therefore did not benefit from the full support they could have given me. Sure, my family was with me all along. With unquestionable compassion they did everything they could to help, but ignorance made them, especially my husband, helpless and frustrated. He tried so hard to help without knowing how, watched my condition deteriorating without being able to do anything to stop it and witnessed my repeated disappointments without having any advice to offer. It is frustrating now to think of how much help he could have given me if only I had the sense to educate him properly.

There was no lack of communication between us. We talked extensively about my problems and about every step that I took or was about to take. I described my suffering and my sensation endlessly, but that was not enough. I, a professional teacher with decades of experience in explaining things to other people, was unable to explain what I was going through. Emotions, sensations and anxieties are not easy to explain, especially when what you need to invoke in the listener are his conscious understanding, not his feelings of compassion.

The simple and obvious solution was staring me in the face all along, but I was too blind to see it. The solution is books. I should have handed my husband one or several books about depression and told him: Read. There is no doubt that through reading he would have not only understood depression far better but would also have found ways to help me actively and effectively.

So my advice on this matter is this: Make them read. Make them read this book, make them read other books, then discuss those books with them. It is easier to discuss the books, not your particular case, and the understanding of your situation will follow automatically.

A properly educated family can help in several ways.

The natural tendency of a person under depression is to retreat from life into an isolated Depressionland, to crawl into a dark cocoon and shut out the world. She does not get out of bed in the morning or sits in a dark room with closed windows and doors. She shuns even the simplest of everyday chores and just wants to be left alone, to brood undisturbed and to nurture depression.

The typical behavior of an uneducated family is to walk on tip-toes, turn down the music or TV and avoid any disturbance. They try not to bother you with anything and to relieve you of any task or responsibility. Pretty soon they get along by themselves, leaving you alone and isolated. They honestly believe that this approach helps, but it is exactly the opposite of what they should be doing.

An educated family will definitely not leave you alone. They will pull you little by little out of isolation and back into a life that is as active as possible under the circumstances. The way to do this is to make you do things, even little things around the house, to come to you for help with homework, to make you walk the dog, anything to keep you involved in what is going on. They should not manage by themselves although they are quite capable of doing so. They should come to you for advice whether they need it or not, and they should let you make decisions. Of course, your family should not try to smash the cocoon with a sledgehammer. That may make things worse. It is better to drill little holes, make some cracks and then keep chipping away, piece by piece, until the holes are big enough and you can come out. Better still, if they catch on early enough they may be able to prevent you from withdrawing into the cocoon in the first place.

Another way that a properly educated family can make a big difference is to help disrupt the vicious circle in your mind.

Our minds play a nasty game with us. The mind amplifies the anxiety caused by depression and then feeds it back to be amplified again, until it gets out of control. In a previous chapter, I used the analogy of a microphone placed close to the loudspeaker. The sound coming out of the loudspeaker is caught by the microphone, amplified by the amplifier and then fed to the loudspeaker again with a much higher intensity, only to be caught again by the microphone and so on. A similar process is happening in your mind, with anxiety instead of sound and with depression serving as the amplifier.

In my case, whenever something made me feel a little better, like a new medication or some progress in work or daily life, it was inevitably accompanied by the worry that the improvement would soon disappear and that I would sink back into my previous condition. That would cause anxiety, which would then be intensified by depression until the anxiety and tensions were so high that I did sink back, all progress wiped out by the vicious circle of amplification and feedback.

My family, especially my husband, saw this process happening time after time, but they were not bold enough or knowledgeable enough to intervene. Had they been better educated about depression they would have been aware of what was happening and could have stepped in to break the cycle.

How can your family intervene? By making you realize what is happening. By making you understand that the amplification of anxiety is only a trick of the depressed mind, with no justification in reality. By giving you a metaphorical slap on the face or pouring a bucket of cold water over your head to snap you out of the vicious circle. By telling you point-blank to cut out the nonsense. It takes some daring to be blunt to a person whose life is obviously in shambles. The natural reaction of a compassionate family is to soothe and commiserate. An educated family would understand what is happening and would be bold enough to take action rather than just watch passively and sympathize.

Armed with a basic knowledge and understanding of depression, an educated family member is in a much better position to assess your situation as it really is. He or she has the tremendous advantage of being able to see things from the outside, with eyes and mind undistorted by depression. Decisions made by a person afflicted with depression are unavoidably made under stress. Such decisions can be easily motivated by a wish for temporary relief and therefore can be biased by how much one is suffering at the moment. It is difficult to think logically and consider objectively all alternatives and their possible consequences with a mind occupied by the fears and anxieties of depression. Your family can help you make those decisions rationally rather than emotionally. Left alone, you may be tossed around in different directions like a small boat adrift on a stormy sea. Your educated family can make your progress more systematic, steering it on a straight course. They can help overcome setbacks and alleviate frustrations and disappointments. Your family can and should be actively involved in all aspects of your campaign against depression.

Your family also can and should be involved in decisions related to doctors and medications, taking an active part in selecting the right doctor and monitoring the effects of new medications. If my own case is any indication, decisions to take or to stop taking medications were often irrational, driven by anxiety and fears invoked by depression. Many such decisions that I made were unnecessary or plainly wrong and produced suffering, frustration and delays. An educated family could have helped me to assess more objectively the effects of each medication and to avoid the unnecessary and harmful switches.

Your family can and should be part of how you restructure your daily life and adjust it to the fight with depression. Your family should help you stay active and busy at all times to keep depression from taking control of your mind. It should pull you out of self imposed isolation and kick you, literally if necessary, into activity whenever you slump into a do-nothing mood.

Your family also can be instrumental in rebuilding your confidence and self-esteem. This will require adjustments in your activities and in what you expect from yourself, to make them compatible with your actual capabilities. Your family should help in this restructuring of your life, and then it should provide you positive feedback for any achievement and encourage you to achieve more.

And, most important, being involved in everything that you do and knowledgeable enough to understand what you should be doing, the educated family will become both your monitor and your guide. They can see, much better than you, what you do right and what you do wrong, what is working and what is not. They can monitor your progress and keep you moving on the right track.

There is a flip side to this coin. You should learn to accept the advice and guidance of your family, knowing that in many ways they are in a better position to make judgments. I know from experience that this is easier said than done. It is much easier to accept advice from someone with authority, someone better informed or more experienced, than from friends and family. After all, why should you accept the guidance of people who obviously have no experience at all, people who only know about the problem from what you tell them and from reading a few books? What do they know at all and how dare they tell you what to do, especially since it is you who must bear the consequences? This "they know nothing" attitude is counterproductive and unfair, to say the least.

The truth is that the people around you, if properly educated, actually are more capable of assessing the situation and of making decisions. They see things more objectively and their judgment is less biased by direct suffering, so they would be less tempted to take the easy ways. On the other hand, you should not accept unconditionally whatever advice your family has to offer. That would be even more counterproductive, because in doing so you would be losing control of your fight with depression and leaving it in the hands of other people. That's something you should never do, even if those other people are your family. The right way is to make evaluations jointly, to discuss everything openly and to take into account the opinions and advice of the family. Then, when the necessary decisions are made, these should be your decisions and you should have the final word in making them.

This education business is a two-way street. Your family must learn about depression to understand what you are going through and how to support you actively. You must learn to trust their judgment, to get them involved in everything that you do or think of doing, and to accept their advice.

There may be some friction at first, because both you and your family have to learn to communicate and to cooperate in ways that most families rarely do. This in itself can tighten the bonds within your family, making it stronger and more united. After awhile, both you and your family will learn to work together as a team and the process will run more smoothly and naturally. When it does, your fight with depression will become much easier and more effective because you will not be in it alone.

EDUCATE YOUR FAMILY
SUMMARY

- Active support from your family and close friends is of paramount importance. Sympathy is not enough.

- To support you effectively your family must be educated about depression.

- It is your job to educate your family.

- The best way to educate them is to make them read.

- An educated family will pull you out of isolation and back into active life.

- An educated family will break the processes that drag you deeper into depression.

- An educated family will help you make decisions rationally and objectively.

Tactic #3
Find the Right Doctor

Doctors cannot cure us of depression; each of us has to do it herself and we can do it without them. So why do we need doctors at all?

We need doctors not because they can cure us of depression but because they can make it easier for us to fight it. We need doctors because in the tug of war with depression in which our mind is playing the part of the rope, doctors can add weight on our side and help us pull harder. We need doctors because, in the inevitable ups and downs of our fight, they can smooth out some of the downs and make them shallower and easier for us to climb out of. We enter the fight at a disadvantage and until we gain momentum and start getting ahead, while all our fighting energy is devoted to just holding on without losing ground, the right doctors can tip the scales in our favor.

I assert so categorically that doctors alone cannot cure depressions for two reasons. First, based on my own experience and on all my reading about the subject, I truly believe that they cannot. I can only express my unprofessional opinion, but almost all authors, including the professionals among them, share that same opinion. The second and more important reason is that to assume anything else, as the natural tendency for wishful thinking would have you do, will jeopardize all prospects of victory.

Nothing is more tempting in times of distress than to put your fate in the hands of someone of authority and then sit back and wait for that someone to solve all your problems. And, it may appear, no one is better suited to solve health problems than an expert doctor. So how can you resist the urge to go to the doctor, pay the bill and wait for him to make depression vanish with the twirl of a magic wand or the flip of a miracle pill? Yield to that temptation and you will remain in the claws of depression for the rest of your life. Yes, medical treatment can relieve some of the hardship. It can make your life more endurable and, after a few years you can even get used to that kind of life and consider it normal. But is that really your goal? Not in my opinion. If all you expect is some relief from the suffering of depression and if you are willing to pay for it by giving up significant parts of your life, medical treatment alone may get you what you want. If you rely only on medical treatment you also should be willing to remain a patient, under constant medical treatment, mainly through psychiatric drugs, for many years, maybe for the rest of your life. But, if your goal is to regain control of your life and live it in full, to do all that you enjoy and to enjoy all that you do, medical treatment alone will not get you there. To count on it to do so is to live under an illusion.

Unfortunately, there are no magic solutions, not even easy solutions. The truth is that no doctor, not even the greatest of experts, should be expected to solve your problem for you. Doctors can be a tremendous help, but it is you who must fight and win. It is both my belief and my experience that you are much better off fighting with the right doctor at your side than without one, provided that you know what can and cannot be expected of him or her.

What cannot and should not be expected of a doctor is an instant solution achieved through medical treatment alone.

What can and should be expected is more difficult to define.

A doctor can and should give you stability and keep you from sinking deeper into depression. Suffering from depression is somewhat like being stuck in quicksand. The quicksand draws in very slowly those who simply accept their fate and remain motionless but tries to pull in faster those who kick and fight. That is because the measures that you take against depression do not necessarily work right away and disappointments are inevitable, especially in the early stages. Your hope that the next step, whatever it is, will actually bring an improvement is often replaced with frustration when it does not. These frustrations build up anxiety, break down your confidence and pull you deeper into the quicksand. Then, the fear of another failure is already built in before you take the next step, raising the likelihood of another disappointment and more frustration. Unlike sinking in quicksand, it is quite possible to fight your way out, but that will be much easier if somebody throws you a rope to hang on to. That somebody is the doctor and the rope is medical treatment. They can keep you from being dragged in by the quicksand, although they cannot pull you out completely. They may even pull you out a bit, so that you are only stuck up to your chest and not up to your chin. Under the circumstances, even that can make a big difference.

In my case, Dr. Sharon's medical treatment was the life vest that kept me afloat. Without it, I might have drowned in depression, never to come out again. Treatment made my depression easier to live with, and in doing so reduced my fears of things to come. The frustrations associated with the fight were still there, but the anxieties they generated were more restrained and I experienced a lesser fear of what the next steps might bring. The knowledge that there was something to hold me up, to keep my condition from spiraling out of control, gave me a sense of confidence and stability. That stability allowed me to carry on the fight.

The first thing to expect from a doctor is stability. He or she should be able to reduce the bad effects of depression to a level you can tolerate and to keep them at or below that level. If your situation is deteriorating and you sink deeper into the quicksand, the doctor should be able to stop the downward motion. Stability provides a solid foothold for the next steps in your fight and the confidence to take those steps. In my case, this stability was achieved mainly through medications. It is reasonable to assume that the same is true in most other cases.

The second thing that the right doctor can and should give you is guidance.

In the war against depression, the soldiers train themselves. There are no officers, no commanders and no instructors. Every single one of us must acquire her war-fighting skills by herself, through learning and mainly through experimentation. You must learn about the enemy and about the means to fight it, then apply those means in practice, discarding those that do not work and retaining those that do. Those means that work you have to refine, learning through trial and error the best ways to apply them in your particular case in the right combinations and dosages.

Nobody can undertake this process of learning, experimentation and refinement for you because nobody but you can tell what works and what does not. Yet, guidance from the right doctor can help a great deal.

A doctor can help in your learning process by pointing out directions, recommending books to read or courses to take. More important, the doctor can and should help establish in your mind the right motivation and attitudes that will nurture your resolve to fight and encourage you along the way. He or she can, and should, help you overcome the doubts and discouragements that will inevitably appear along the way, suggest a change of direction when you get stuck and help you assess your progress. The doctor can also recommend techniques and exercises for you to learn and try.

Your doctor possesses two extremely powerful assets, in addition to medical expertise, that he or she must use to accelerate your progress towards victory over depression. Doctors have a tremendous amount of cumulative experience at their disposal, both personal experience with many other people and institutional experience accumulated in hospitals, universities and research institutes. You, on the other hand, have nothing but your own experience. The right doctor will find a way to give you the benefit of all this experience through his or her guidance and advice.

The other asset is your trust. Fighting depression alone often feels like walking on thin ice, without knowing whether the next step will bring you closer to victory or plunge you into the cold water of failure and disappointment. Everything that you do is essentially new and quite demanding, while your confidence is eroded by the sufferings of depression and by the disappointments and failures that have occurred along the way. In these circumstances, trust in someone with knowledge, experience and authority is the best substitute for confidence in yourself. The right doctor will gain your trust and then turn it into an abundant source of encouragement and motivation for you.

In my opinion, a doctor that does not use these assets to push you forwards is simply not doing his or her job properly.

Probably the most demanding thing that the right doctor should do for you is to provide continuous support in the fight. By that I mean that the doctor should be always available when needed, whenever depression gains the upper hand, whenever you feel that you are losing ground, whenever the things you try to do fail to work, whenever you need encouragement and hope.

Nothing can provide you more peace of mind and confidence than the certainty that you can always count on someone you trust to be there when needed. By being there, I mean available on the phone and willing to talk, ready to make an appointment when you ask for it and not a week from next Tuesday, always ready with some words of encouragement that make sense and do not make you feel like a child. A serious discussion that convinces you that you are actually doing fine when things appear to go all wrong, a telephone conversation that fills you with hope when you are close to despair, a suggestion on how to proceed when nothing seems to be working, all these can do wonders if they come when really needed.

To live up to these expectations, your doctor must believe that the solution to depression is in your hands, not in his. Your doctor must believe that you are the one doing the fighting and that he should provide support and create the conditions for the fight to be successful. Your doctor must also believe in your ability to conduct the fight.

When you find the doctor that does all that, you will know that you have found the Right Doctor.

I keep referring to the "right doctor", not just the "doctor", and with good reason.

Any competent doctor should be able to prescribe the medications that have the potential to stabilize your condition. But that is definitely not enough, not even as far as medications are concerned. For any medication to be effective, the person who takes it should not resist but rather cooperate with the medication. If my case is any indication, just taking medications without having a frame of mind that is willing to accept them can lead to very negative consequences. Even when a medication made me feel better, worries about side effects and fears that the improvement would soon fade away would settle in and negate the effect of the medication to the point that I actually felt worse for taking it. I will elaborate on this issue in the next chapter, but let me just emphasize that it is up to the doctor to create in you that state of mind that will make the treatment accepted and effective. If, as so many doctors did in my case, your doctor merely prescribes the medication and, when it does not work, prescribes another one, he or she is not the right doctor for you. Find another.

The qualities that make a doctor the Right Doctor are high expectations. They are also quite subjective; their fulfillment strongly depends on both personalities involved and on the compatibility of these personalities. Your trust in your doctor must go far beyond your trust in an expert professional. Your doctor must also believe in you and in your ability to persevere and win. These expectations go far beyond professional competence and require from the doctor a commitment that many doctors are reluctant or unable to make. Even those that are willing to make such a commitment can probably make it only selectively, not to all their patients. Therefore, a doctor that does not live up to those expectations is not a bad doctor; in fact, he or she can be an excellent doctor but not the Right Doctor, not the one that is right for you.

Your search for the right doctor may be long and tedious, as it was in my case, but when at last you do find the one you are looking for it will be more than worth the effort. In my case it was the turning point, the beginning of victory. So, do not give up and do not compromise. Keep searching for your Right Doctor.

FIND THE RIGHT DOCTOR
SUMMARY

- Medical treatment alone will not cure depression, but doctors can make it easier for us to fight it.

- The right doctor should provide stability, a solid foothold and the confidence to go on fighting.

- The right doctor should provide guidance, encouragement, motivation and attitudes that will nurture your determination and your perseverance.

- The right doctor should provide peace of mind by being be there for you whenever needed.

- Fulfillment of these expectations strongly depends on both personalities involved and on their ability to establish mutual trust.

- Keep searching for your right doctor. Do not give up and do not compromise.

Tactic #4
Medications are a Non-Issue

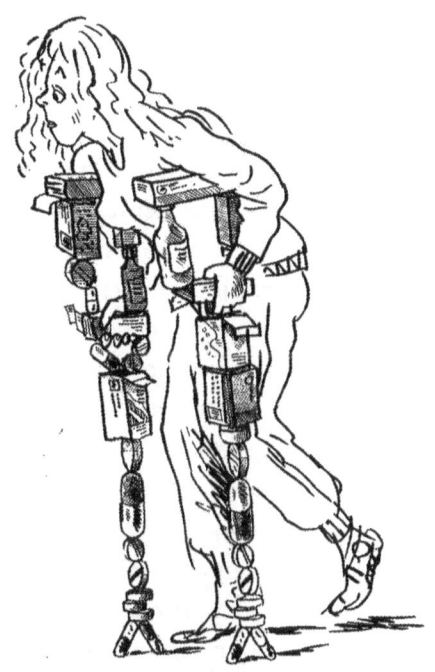

If you browse through books on depression and related subjects on bookstore shelves, and especially if you read some of the books, it becomes obvious that medications are a big issue. There are many books written on anti-depressant medications (about one of them in particular) and the issue has a place of honor in many other books.

To some authors, mainly health professionals but others as well, medications are not everything when it comes to treating depression, they are the only thing. Other authors, health professionals as well, go as far as to accuse the drug manufacturing industry of a conspiracy, no less, in collaboration with psychiatrists, to induce the unsuspecting public to take more anti-depressant drugs than really needed. Of course, there are many shades of gray between these extremes, but they all have one thing in common: medications are a big issue.

Medications do not deserve a chapter in this book. What I had to say about them in other contexts could have been enough. The only reason I include this chapter is to make this point: Medications are a non-issue.

As I mentioned earlier, medications are to depression what crutches are to a broken leg. They can help you get around and make life more bearable but they do not cure depression any more than the crutches cure the leg. Medications can help us get by until the other things that we do to fight depression take effect. They can stabilize our condition and prevent it from getting worse, and that is no small matter. But that is all. They can do no more. Relying on medications to get you out of depression is a big mistake because they simply cannot. To rely on them to the exclusion of everything else is to commit yourself to a lifetime of hobbling on crutches.

On the other hand, resisting medications is also a big mistake. Some people, me included, have an anti-medication attitude. It may be simple fear of an unknown factor; it may be concern about possible side effects or just plain rejection of external interference in our body. Whatever the cause of this attitude, it makes us turn medications into a big issue.

In my case, the concern about taking drugs, especially when I did not particularly trust the doctors who had prescribed them, filled my mind with unnecessary anxieties and dominated my attention. Instead of devoting my attention and whatever energy I could muster to the things I could do to fight depression, I wasted that energy and a lot of time worrying about pills and what they might do to me. As a result, I rejected even those pills that did work and made me feel good, only to be replaced by other pills that fared no better. So I lost not only time but also the benefits that medications could have provided. I lost the stability they should have created and suffered more than I should have, and for no real reason. My anti-medication attitude even drove me deeper into depression by the extra anxiety and fears it created.

What I should have done was to take those pills and forget about them, never to give them another thought. I should have used whatever support and stability the pills could offer to do the things that could really advance my fight. And, if I could not do that alone, somebody should have forced me to. Somebody should have told me to take those pills and stop all the nonsense of worrying about them (here comes the educated family again). Unfortunately, nobody did.

So the point is this: If you need crutches, if you can get along better with them than without them, fine. Go ahead, use those crutches; it makes no sense not to. Take the medications and do not give them another thought. They are not the issue, they are not the solution and they are not the problem, they are just crutches.

MEDICATIONS ARE A NON-ISSUE
SUMMARY

- It is a big mistake to rely on medications to get you out of depression. They cannot.

- It is a big mistake to resist medications. It makes no sense not to use medications if you can get along better with them than without them.

- So take the medications if necessary and do not give them another thought.

- Medications are not the issue, they are not the solution and they are not the problem, they are just crutches.

Tactic #5
Keep Busy

"Cogito, ergo sum". I think, therefore I am. That was how the French philosopher Descartes proved his own existence. "**You** think, therefore **I** am" would be a suitable way for depression to prove that it exists. Depression exists in my mind as a thought process. Depression is my thoughts gone berserk. I think, therefore **it** exists. My thoughts have created depression, my thoughts keep it alive and my thoughts feed it. Take my thoughts away, deprive depression of their nourishment, and it will soon wither and dry up.

Depression is a malfunction of the mind, a cycle of anxiety intensified by the mind to create a bigger anxiety, then intensified again and again. A hostile force has invaded my mind and strives to take control of my thoughts and to keep this self-destructive cycle going. Even if unable to drive the invader out, I am still capable of fighting it for control of my own thoughts. If I win this fight, if I break the cycle, the invader has no power over me.

The straightforward way to deprive depression of my thoughts is simply to think about something else. If my mind is occupied with other things, if my thoughts are focused on something else, depression cannot control them. This may sound simple, but it is really not simple at all. It is nearly impossible for anybody to take control of his or her thoughts directly, by a deliberate act of will, especially when depression is pulling on them in the opposite direction. So, an indirect strategy should be employed. Fortunately, such a strategy is readily available and not so difficult to implement.

The strategy is to reduce the share of the mind's time taken up by depression.

The tactics are to fill the mind with as many tasks as possible, so that even if each task takes only a small share of the mind's time, together they will take up a significant portion.

The method is to keep busy, very busy, to keep the mind occupied with things other than the anxiety of depression.

The premise for this strategy is that while the mind is busy with other things it cannot think the thoughts that become depression.

I do not claim that the mind can think of only one thing at a time. This statement, even if true, would be misleading. Even if the mind cannot think of A while it is thinking of B, left to itself it can very easily drift from A to B and to C and to D. When the mind is afflicted with depression, it will tend to drift from anything to D, D for Depression, that is. Every one of us experiences this wandering of the mind many times every day, and no intentional mental effort is really capable of stopping it for very long. I prefer to think that the mind, like most computers, handles many thoughts on a time-sharing basis, switching from one to the other either under deliberate control or in response to some external stimulus. Very often it switches apparently on its own accord, driven by some internal processes that we are not really aware of and certainly cannot control. The mind performs many thought-tasks that are constantly competing with each other for their share of the mind's time. Depression must compete with all the other tasks that are active in the mind at any given time. When you are busy doing something that requires your mind's attention, the mind is busy with whatever you are doing and cannot devote much of its time, or maybe none at all, to depression. On the other hand, when you are idle your mind is also idle so that depression can monopolize your thoughts and exclude all other tasks from the competition.

Everything that you do, even the most mundane activity, requires some attention. You must pay some attention even to humdrum jobs like washing dishes, shopping for groceries or working out in the gym. It is impossible to have any kind of interaction with other people without the mind taking some part in it. And, every bit of time and attention that the mind devotes to any activity is -salvaged from the jaws of depression. Every activity bites into depression's share of your mind-time and reduces its stranglehold on your thoughts. Every such bite brings you a little bit closer to your objective. The key is to do things and to do them all the time, to keep busy every possible moment by hook or by crook.

"Do things," I say, but what things? Actually, it does not really matter. Whatever keeps you active and your mind occupied is fine. One thing matters and one thing only: do not allow yourself to be idle, not for a moment. Idleness is the traitor within you that throws the gates of your mind wide open for depression to come in and take over, whereas your objective is to keep depression out. When you are busy, the mind is busy and has no time for the thoughts of depression. When you are not busy, neither is the mind, so your thoughts are free to roam unrestrained. When they do, the anxieties and fears that are depression take over and fill up the mind in no time.

Anyone who is familiar with depression is also familiar with the inevitable tendency to do nothing. Everything becomes very difficult, nothing is worth making an effort for and there is no energy to make the effort anyway. When the mind is drained of energy and the will paralyzed, the natural consequence is to do nothing, to be idle. Depression produces idleness and idleness induces depression. But, fortunately, the reverse is also true. Avoid idleness and you drive depression out, keep busy and you liberate your mind and yourself from its oppression. So you must overcome the tendency to do nothing and keep busy in spite of depression.

But how does one keep busy in spite of depression? One can conceivably fill up a day with activities done just for the sake of doing something at all. There is nothing wrong with that because even such activities can occupy the mind and achieve the objective of biting off chunks of mind-time and attention. The problem is that we are talking now of a process that will take many months, maybe years. One can fill up no more than a few days with activities that have no purpose, and then what? What I recommend, in fact what I very strongly urge you to do is much more ambitious, also infinitely more effective in more ways than one. Most important, it works and you can do it.

What you should do are the same things, and all the things that you did before depression. Work, sports, hobbies, social life, love life, all the things that life is made of, without giving up anything, without ever thinking: "I cannot do this" or "What is the use of doing that?" Yes, depression does make a big difference between what you can do now and what you could do before. But that difference is in the intensity and duration of what you can do, not in the basic capability of doing things. It is a difference of degree, not a Yes or No. Being depressed does not mean that you are incapable of doing the same things you did before. It only means that you can do them with lesser intensity and for shorter periods of time.

For example, if you think that putting in a full day's work is too difficult, why not work for half a day or just for two or three hours? If I thought that I could not play tennis for three hours a day as I had before, why did I not just play for half an hour every day? Depression does not deprive us of our mental or physical abilities. It did not take away my ability to teach mathematics and it cannot take away your ability to do your work, whatever that may be. Depression did not make me physically unable to play tennis and it cannot make it physically impossible for you to engage in whatever activity you prefer. It cannot take away our ability to do things, only our ability to want to do them and our confidence in being able to do them. The difference between doing something in spite of depression and giving it up because of depression lies in the motivation. Given the right incentive or the right circumstances, you can perform the normal activities of your life and while doing so weaken the grip of depression. Without motivation, you give up, stop doing one thing after another and succumb to idleness, which only strengthens depression's grip on you.

Let me once again use my own case to illustrate what I mean. I worked before depression hit and I worked all the time that I was under its yoke. Work was more difficult, especially when I had to work more than two or three hours a day, but it was not impossible. I could work even during the most difficult of times. On the other hand, I did give up some other things that were very important to me, even tennis. But what was the difference? Why was I capable of working and not capable of playing tennis?

Had anybody asked me at that time why I did not play, the answer would have certainly been "because I cannot play!" Was it true that I could not play? Certainly not. The truth is that I was afraid to play, afraid of not being able to measure up to my usual performance level, afraid of facing the members of my club. Even if playing for hours would have been too difficult, there was nothing to prevent me from playing for shorter periods of time or against lesser opponents. Nothing, except for my fears. When I did play with

Rotem, my daughter, those same fears would make me stop after fifteen minutes or so.

But if asked: "How can you teach?" My answer would have been, "I must teach." I had an obligation to the school and to the kids, so not teaching was not really an option. Teaching was not less difficult or less demanding than playing tennis. If anything, it was more demanding in many ways. But somehow I felt that I must teach, so I did it. I did not feel that I must play tennis, so I let myself believe that I was unable to play and actually stopped playing.

Although teaching did require an effort, it should have taught me something that I understood only much later. While standing in front of those kids and teaching, I was feeling good, relatively speaking of course. Sure, it took a great physical and mental effort to stand and teach but while doing so I was relatively free of the anxieties that were haunting me at any other time. Of course I noticed the absence of tensions while I was teaching, but I failed to realize that the grip of depression loosened because my mind was occupied with mathematics and my attention was focused on the kids. Had I understood that, I might have also understood that this was true not just for teaching but for any other activity as well.

I let myself believe that I could not possibly do so many things that had been part of my life before depression, such as playing tennis, working out in the gym, going shopping, meeting friends, going on vacation, the list goes on and on. So, I gave it all up. True, it was much more difficult to engage in any of these activities than it had been before depression and there is no doubt that I would have enjoyed them a lot less, if at all, but that is beside the point. The point is that I should have made an effort to do each and every one of those things just as I made an effort to teach. I should have made the effort not for the sake of enjoying those activities but for the sake of just doing them and for the sake of being busy doing them. Of course, the objective difficulties of my mental and physical condition at that time would have imposed strict limitations on how much, how long and how well I could do things. So what? I could have done every activity in small doses, a little bit at a time, and then a little bit more and again a little bit more. There is no doubt that had I done that for tennis instead of giving it up, I would have been able to play more and better as time went by. More important, there is no doubt that I would have felt better and better while playing, just as I felt better while teaching.

I keep saying "I should have" and "I could have" because unfortunately for me, I did not realize all this until a late stage in my fight. Only then did I understand what a big mistake I had made in allowing myself to give up so much of my life. I urge you not to do the same mistake.

Look back on your life in recent years. What have you given up? What has become too difficult or simply not worth the effort of doing? Is it work? A hobby? Sports? Spending time with your family? Social life? Every woman has her equivalent of my tennis; everybody has things that matter, things that are important and enjoyable. It is a big mistake to give them up because of depression. One must make the effort to keep doing those things, as difficult as it may be.

Force yourself to do it, whatever your "thing" may be, if only for a few minutes at a time. Force yourself to ignore the difficulty, forget the "I cannot do this" nonsense and just do it. Soon it will become less difficult and even enjoyable again, and you will feel much better for doing it. This is where an educated family can make the difference. If they understand what is happening and what a mistake it is to give up doing what is important to you, they can, in fact they should, give you the push and the encouragement to do it. Had my husband been properly educated about depression at the time he should have literally dragged or kicked me out onto the tennis court every day.

The basic message is this: Do not give up any of your normal-life activities because of depression. You are just as capable as ever of doing everything that you do. Depression cannot take that away. It can only make things more difficult to do. So, if necessary, do less of the activities that are too difficult to do in full but do them nonetheless.

While you are busy with those activities, depression is pushed aside, which inevitably relieves the bad feelings, anxieties and pressures that depression makes you feel. In other words, being busy will make you feel better, as simple as that. And, as time goes by the difficulties caused by depression will diminish and you will again be able to do in full those things that you could only do less of.

This brings up the issue of filling the gaps. On one hand, it is important to be busy all the time so that the mind is occupied with other thoughts and keeps depression out. On the other hand, even if you keep doing all your normal-life activities such as work and sports that filled your days before, you will probably be doing most things part-time, which will leave gaps in your daily routine. These gaps are dangerous because even if you drive depression out of your thoughts while you are busy with other things, it is still there, waiting for any opportunity to break in. It will take advantage of any opening, be it an open door or a small crack, to infiltrate your mind with bad thoughts and take it over.

There are two things to do about this issue. First and foremost, accept it for what it is. Accept it as a fact of life that no matter how busy you are, it is not practically possible to keep depression out of your mind 100% of the time. There will be times every day when it breaks through your defenses or sneaks in through some back door. This is nothing to worry about. As long as you know that it is in your power to do something that will drive depression back out of our mind, you need not fear. You can get busy again or you can apply the thought methods that I will discuss in the next chapters. So what if your mind is suddenly filled with bad thoughts and anxieties? Trust that they soon will be gone. You know how to make them go away, and you shall make them go away. The knowledge that once you get busy again you will feel better and the bad thoughts will be gone should be in itself sufficient to relieve your fears and reduce your anxiety. So, even when depression does get a hold of you, you are no longer entirely at its mercy. You know that its hold is temporary and will soon be gone. You know that you are still in control.

The other thing to do is to fill in the gaps as much as possible. Those periods between activities should not become times of idleness. You should not spend your evenings slumped in front of the TV doing nothing. I discovered that it is always possible to find something to do, such as going for a walk, doing house chores, reading a book, checking my bills and bank account, playing the piano, preparing exercises for the next day's classes, anything to stay busy, even during those times when other people are normally idle. It is not easy to stay busy when you are tired and both your mind and your body desire their well-earned rest. The trouble is that there can be no real rest because the moment you become idle, the bad thoughts take over, anxiety builds up and rest eludes you, no matter how tired you are. If peace and quiet are not really an option, the choice is between the bad feelings of depression while doing nothing and the effort of doing something to avoid being idle. Whenever possible, choose the second alternative.

Being busy all the time is not easy. But, as with most things, the name of the game is to go slowly and stay with it. Whenever a task is too difficult to do in full, it helps to break it down into smaller tasks and do just one small piece at a time. After awhile, it becomes possible to do a little bit more and then another little bit and another. It also helps to do several tasks in parallel, switching from one to another when you get tired. For example, after working for ten or fifteen minutes at the computer I used to get up and do something around the house. Then I would come back to the computer for awhile, and so on.

It is very useful to build a rigid daily routine, to set up fixed times and durations for everything you plan to do during the day and to stick to them meticulously. If you know in advance every day what you are going to do and when, the temptation of idleness and the excuse of being tired are much easier to overcome.

The sensation of being drained of energy, like a deflated basketball, is one of the trademarks of depression. It is what depression makes you feel and think about yourself, but like everything else related to depression these feelings are not an objective truth. They are only a perception, a subjective image, an artifact of the bad thoughts in your mind. Being active and staying busy is the best and most effective way to get rid of these sensations and regain control.

This whole process of doing your normal-life activities without giving anything up and then filling in the gaps to stay busy at all times is no piece of cake. It takes effort and determination, but it can be done and it works. The good news is that it works right from the start. There is no need to wait for long before you feel an improvement. Everything that you do, every bit of activity that you add to your daily life, makes you feel better right away. Once you realize that, making the next effort becomes much easier.

And, you must always consider the alternative. The alternative is to give in to depression and suffer all the consequences. The way I see it, there really is no choice.

KEEP BUSY
SUMMARY

- If your thoughts are focused on something else, depression cannot control them. So keep busy to keep the mind occupied.

- Depression monopolizes your mind when it is idle. Do not allow yourself to be idle.

- Do not give up any of your normal-life activities. If a task is too difficult to do in full, break it down into smaller tasks and do them one at a time.

- Depression cannot take away your ability to do things. So ignore the difficulty, forget the "I cannot do this" nonsense and just do it. Soon it will become less difficult and you will feel much better for doing it.

- Build a rigid daily routine and stick to it.

Tactic #6
Control Bad Thoughts

If depression is the enemy, bad thoughts are its troops and its agents. They are the channels through which depression infiltrates and conquers your mind. Bad thoughts are the instruments depression uses to take control of your life. In your fight against depression, you have to tackle the bad thoughts and block their way into your mind.

No single course of action can defeat bad thoughts; there is no single tactic that you can rely on to do the job. You must employ a combination of means and tactics. Keeping busy is one such tactic, but it must not be the only one because you cannot possibly keep the bad thoughts out all the time, no matter how busy you manage to stay.

Other tactics will address the bad thoughts directly, not build a detour around them, as the keeping-busy tactic does. First, you must identify those thoughts and understand the mechanisms that produce them. It is not at all difficult to become aware of the presence of those bad thoughts in your mind. That is because they make their presence felt through physical and mental phenomena that each of us is all too familiar with. But being aware of the presence of bad thoughts is not enough. You must also learn to identify what causes them and understand how it does so.

Now what are those bad thoughts of depression? Every one of us has her own batch of them. I can only describe my own, but I believe they are not uncommon.

First and foremost: fear and stress. These two states are so tightly connected that it is impossible to address them separately.

For me it was mostly a fear of feeling bad, a fear of the pressures and tensions of depression or, one might say, a fear of depression itself. At any time, even when I was feeling well and had no reason to expect feeling otherwise, I would suddenly find my mind filled with a fear of those hateful pressures in the head. At first there was no perceptible reason for those fears. They just materialized in my mind, out of nowhere. And, when they did, I invariably began to feel bad, to feel those same pressures and tensions that I dreaded. The fear of feeling bad actually made me feel bad. But later, as I got more familiar with my depression through reading and experience, I came to realize that in many cases those fears did not come out of nowhere, that they had causes.

One cause was stress and the anticipation of stress. Every person's life comes with many built-in sources of stress. Work, family, money matters, interactions with other people and just the world we live in can cause stress that every one of us experiences every day of his or her life. Stress is a part of life and no one can avoid it. One can only endure and overcome it, which is what most people do all the time. But we who have depression are less capable of coping with stress. For us, it becomes a main source of fear and suffering.

I think of this as a threshold mechanism, similar to that of the pain threshold, which is different from person to person. If you inflict the same pain, say by cutting the skin in the same place with the same knife, to a person with a high pain threshold and to another with a low pain threshold, the first person may hardly notice the cut while to the other person it will be very painful. By the same token, if two people, one with a high stress threshold and one with a low stress threshold, are exposed to the same stressful situation, the first may experience a minor annoyance while the other will suffer the consequences of intense stress. Depression lowers the tress threshold drastically, so what may cause only a minor irritation or even go unnoticed for a non-depressed person becomes a source of major stress, anxiety and tension to a person suffering from depression.

Stresses in my family worked that way for me. Fortunately, there are no problems in my family life today and there never have been. But like every family, we do experience small and inevitable frictions. Before depression, a disagreement about the purchase of some item for the house or my annoyance with my husband or children for forgetting to do something would be history after a few minutes or a few hours. Under depression, such minor irritations could cause significant amounts of stress that would inevitably make me suffer from tensions and pressures for days. The irritation was the same as before and the other people involved were definitely the same. Only my stress threshold was much lower because of my depression.

Likewise, when caught in situations that made me feel ill at ease or when trapped in uncomfortable circumstances that I could not control, I would become uptight and restless. Then pressures and tension would build up in no time.

The situations I am talking about were quite harmless and common. Perhaps it was having lunch with a friend, when I would have to sit for an hour or so and trade small talk and gossip, or maybe attending a family reunion, which was much worse because it lasted longer and involved more people. Sometimes it was just going somewhere by car, when after twenty or thirty minutes I would be desperate just to stop the car and get out, or a teachers' meeting that seemed to last forever, flooded with endless talk, only fifteen minutes after it had started.

There was nothing new about how I felt about those situations. I had hated them just as much before suffering from depression. Small talk had always bored me, long and verbose meetings had always annoyed me and long trips had always caused discomfort and irritation. Stressful situations had always been stressful and they still are. The difference was in my ability to endure the stress. Stresses that before depression had been nothing more than small and temporary nuisances became real problems. Depression magnified the intensity of stress out of proportion to the situation that caused it. And, I had lost the capacity to ignore the nuisances or to tolerate and overcome them.

Usually, the pressures did not wait for me to get into those situations. They anticipated them and showed up in advance. Or rather, I anticipated the situation and just thinking about it created the pressures. So, knowing in advance that I would be in a stressful situation and knowing that when that happened I would feel bad, induced tension and fear. That fear would produce the same bad feeling I was afraid of in the first place.

As if being unable to cope with my own problems was not bad enough, depression also turned the problems of others into a major source of stress for me. I had always been involved in everything around me and saw everybody's problems as mine to solve. Everything that had to do with the children was my concern, as were all family matters, all financial matters, my husband's health problems, problems in the schools where I worked, problems at the tennis club where I played and everything else in sight. I took the weight of every problem and every responsibility upon my shoulders and had no difficulty in carrying the burden. In fact, it was not really a burden at all until depression took hold of me. With depression, the load was still there on my shoulders but my ability to carry it was gone. I could no longer cope with the problems of others, but at the same time I was unable to ignore them and take their load off my shoulders.

The truth was that there was no need for me to carry that load anymore. My children, my husband and everybody else were quite capable of handling their problems without me and nobody really expected me, in my obviously bad condition, to worry about anything beside my own problems. But my mind, weighted down with depression, was blind to this objective truth. It refused to give up the burden of other people's problems, although it was fully aware that it could not handle them. The result of all this was unavoidable: more stress.

Taking medications also was a plentiful source of stress and fear. Each new medication came with a built-in set of unknown factors and each such factor was a source of fear. Initially, I was afraid that the medication would do no good. Then I feared the side effects, or that the dosage was too high or too low. Psychiatric medications typically take a week or two before their effects can be felt. For me, those periods of waiting were packed with fears and with the stress and bad feeling that fear produced. New fears showed up when the medications finally did take effect. If the medication made me feel better, I feared that the improvement would soon disappear and the bad feeling would return. If it did not make me feel better, I feared that continuing to take it would cause all sorts of bad effects. In both cases my negative attitude towards medications made me afraid of becoming fully dependent on them. This sequence repeated itself methodically every time, with two inevitable results. First, the medication did not have any chance of success and would soon be replaced by another. Second, the whole period was filled with stress and sensations of intense pressures and tensions, which is just what the medications were intended to relieve in the first place.

My worst fear was also the most justified. That was the fear of what was happening to me and of never being able to get back to my previous life. This fear was genuine, not an artifact of my mind like the others, but it was a direct result of depression nonetheless. Depression is frightening, and with good reason. A woman leading a full, active, satisfying and happy life finds herself drowning in quicksand, sinking deeper and deeper every day with no hope of rescue in sight. How can that not scare her to death?

Falling from normal life into depression is like being thrown into another world. Things in this world behave differently than in the world where we have lived all our life, as if governed by different laws of nature. What would cause a certain effect in the old world causes an entirely different and often unpredictable effect in the new world. The one thing that is predictable is that the effect will be bad and will make us suffer. The unknown world and the pain we constantly encounter in it inspire fear, not only of what we are actually experiencing but also of what we imagine that we might experience. That fear makes us create our own monsters, just as a child who is afraid of the dark imagines fearful creatures that are not really there and then fears these creatures more than he fears the dark. Fear of the real and imaginary bad creatures are one and the same in our mind, although one inspires the other.

The key to reducing your fears and putting them under control is to learn about this world of depression that you live in and to adapt to it. Once you become more familiar with this world and begin to understand how it works, your fear of the unknown will diminish. You will begin to realize that the monsters you were afraid of are imaginary creations of your mind. Then it becomes possible to understand the mechanisms that produce these fears and devise ways to deal with them.

The solution to my fears began with the understanding that they were coming from stressful situations and from the anticipation of such situations. Whenever I felt the pressures mounting in my head, I would try to find their source. I would think about what I was doing at the time and what I was going to do in the next few days and try to identify potential sources of discomfort, tension, boredom, irritation or any other bad feeling. Then I would try to find ways to reduce or eliminate those sources.

This process of identification and containment, of finding and isolating the sources of stress one by one, then figuring out ways to restrain and if possible eliminate each one of them, is still going on for me. It started as a one-step-at-a-time process that gradually picked up steam and eventually led to a significant change in my attitude, my outlook on life and the way I live it. This process and the new attitude that it has created are among the main reasons for my being able to think of depression in the past tense.

Depression makes you look at problems through powerful binoculars, making any problem appear big, very close and menacing. Because you have a low stress threshold, most problems, even those that are objectively trivial, pass the threshold and cause significant stress. This stress then causes anxiety and fear, which amplifies the problem, only to cause more stress and so on. To break this cycle, you must turn the binoculars around and make the problem look small and far away. Viewed that way, the problems will not produce nearly as much stress as when they loom over you big and close.

There are several ways to turn the binoculars around. First, you can try to look at the problem objectively and evaluate it for what it is really worth, not as what the amplification of depression would make it seem. As will be evident from the examples that follow, many of the problems that had caused me a lot of stress were, when viewed objectively, really insignificant, maybe even trivial. Once I managed to cut them down to their actual size, they were no longer problems. A second way is to break the problem into small fragments and to look at each piece separately. If each fragment is small enough to brush off as a non-issue, the sum of all fragments is not a problem any more. And, you can minimize a problem by looking at it from a different angle and thinking of the glass as being half full, not half empty. In most cases you will discover that you are dealing with issues that in reality are not as bad as depression would make you believe. It is often possible to find a bright side to the problem or to see how temporary and insignificant it is simply by asking whether it will still be a problem tomorrow or next week.

These are generalities, I know, but they have to be because each of us is looking at her particular set of stress-producing problems and must reverse the binoculars on each and every one of them individually. Here is how I reversed the binoculars on some of mine.

The solution to fear and stress caused by medications came when I understood that medications were a non-issue and learned to take them and never to give them a second thought.

The solution to stress caused by shouldering the problems of others came from the understanding that there was no need for me to solve these problems or even worry about them. Whenever I traced my stress to this cause, I would ask myself whether it was really a problem and if it was, whether it would still be a problem a week or a month later. It turned out that most such problems were temporary and would be either resolved by themselves or simply gone within a short while, so there was no sense in worrying about them. For those problems that remained, I would ask myself whether the person involved was incapable of handling it without me. If the answer was no, which it almost always was, I would try to separate myself from that problem and stop worrying and even thinking about it. And so, piece by piece, I managed to remove the load from my shoulders and get rid of the stresses it had produced.

When I identified an upcoming social or family event as the source of my anxiety, I would plan to come late or find some excuse to leave early. During the event I would find ways to move around: step outdoors if possible, go and help in the kitchen whether help was needed or not, play with the children if there were any or just do anything to avoid being stuck in one place. Knowing in advance that there were things I would be able to do to reduce the stress and planning those things eliminated my fear of the anticipated event and the stress and pressures it would have caused. After a while I became so practiced in finding things to do during social and family events that they no longer bothered me at all.

If the source of my stress was some friction with my husband, I would think about the issue that had caused that friction and try to convince myself that it was really insignificant, which it usually really was. I also learned to identify those frictions in advance and to avoid them in the first place. Before depression, I had no reservations about getting into an argument whenever there was a difference of opinion on almost anything. The cost of such arguments was low and affordable because they would be done with and forgotten in a short while. With depression, the cost of arguments became high because they resulted in a build-up of stress, automatically followed by pressures in the head that made me suffer for days. The arguments were simply not worth the price. I believe that the people around me, particularly my husband, also realized what a stiff price arguments and frictions were exacting from me and made their best effort to avoid them.

Similarly, I learned to identify the situations that were causing stress at work and in every other aspect of my life. Then I found ways to reduce the stress in each situation. That was a slow and gradual process, consisting of many small steps. Each step dealt with a specific source of stress and with the ways to eliminate or avoid the source and to reduce the stress and fear it produced. Once I got started, the process was almost mechanical, one step leading to another and each step easier than its predecessor. Having identified and dealt with one source of stress and fear, it became easier to identify the next one, simply because one more source had been taken out of the game. The experience I had gained in previous steps made dealing with any newly identified source simpler and faster.

And, most important, the solution to the fears of depression itself began with the realization that the things I did to get rid of the various sources of fear and stress were working.

Stepping back from the canvas to see the whole picture rather than the brush strokes, I realize that this process has changed my entire life. By a gradual evolution driven by necessity, it has changed my attitude toward many things in life, as well as my way of thinking and living. It would have been impossible to achieve these changes by revolution, driven either by some flash of enlightenment or by decree of some doctor (or should I say Guru?). It came from within, from very practical and essentially quite ad hoc measures taken to relieve the hateful pressures in my head and to diminish the stresses and fears that depression strived to magnify. Yet, looking back from where I am today, I believe that this process of stress reduction by identifying and restraining the things that made me feel fear and stress has changed my entire life for the better.

I believe that every person, not only those who suffer from depression, should embark on a stress reduction process and change his or her life in the same manner. The only difference, in this context, between a person who suffers from depression and one who does not is the level of their stress threshold. People with depression have lower thresholds than the others but the stress is the same and everybody's life will be better and more enjoyable with less stress.

For those of us who have to live with depression, stress reduction is not only a way out but also a way of life. No matter what we do and how well we manage to overcome depression and to live a full, active and enjoyable life, we cannot raise our stress threshold. It will always remain low, so we must constantly keep the level of stress below that threshold. If we fail to do so, depression is always there, waiting for a chance to come back.

I continue to apply the same process of identification and containment of sources of stress on a routine basis. It has become second nature for me and I do it all the time. The good news is that practice and experience have made this an effortless process.

I feel that people around me, mainly my family, have also adjusted their behavior to help with my ongoing stress-reduction process. It may be deliberate on their part or they may just be going along with what I do, but they do help create a low stress environ-ment for me and, through me, also for themselves.

CONTROL BAD THOUGHTS
SUMMARY

- Depression lowers your stress threshold. What is a minor irritation to another person becomes a major source of stress to you.

- You cannot raise the stress threshold, so you must keep the level of stress below it.

- Stress reduction is a process of finding and isolating the sources of stress, then finding ways to restrain or eliminate each source.

- Depression makes you look at problems through binoculars, so any problem appears big and menacing. Turn the binoculars around and make the problem look small and far away.

- Try to look at each problem objectively and evaluate it for what it really is, not as what depression would make it seem.

- Break the problem into fragments, each small enough to brush off as a non-issue, and the entire problem will fade away.

- Minimize a problem by looking at it from different angles. Will it still be a problem tomorrow?

Tactic #7
Rebuild Confidence

Depression and confidence come and go together. When one comes, the other goes. The onset of depression is often accompanied by the loss of confidence, while the regaining of confidence is part and parcel of getting rid of depression.

It is not quite clear whether depression causes a loss of confidence or whether the loss of confidence precedes depression and helps bring it about. To me, both statements are true to some extent. A loss of confidence can be traced to true-life situations that many people experience with or without depression, so depression is not entirely to blame. On the other hand, depression makes us feel helpless and frustrated, which shatters our self-assurance to pieces.

The phase of our lives commonly referred to as midlife, typically around the age of fifty, produces changes in our lives that some find hard to cope with. Most of our goals in life have either already been achieved or will probably never be achieved. Our children are grown up and gone on their own ways, which generally takes them away from us in more ways than one. This is also the age when many of us have to deal with health problems. Progress at work or in our careers slows down or stops, leaving us more or less stationary, sometimes overtaken by younger people. And for us women, on top of every-thing else, at menopause our bodies become strangers to us and seem to betray us.

These changes in our lives are real, not imaginary, and none of them is a change for the better. They happen, or at least some of them do, to almost every person in this age group. When they do, you may feel that your life has become empty, that the significance of life and the appetite for it have both diminished. This sensation of emptiness and the loss of self-esteem that often comes along with it make us feel unsure of ourselves. We lose our confidence and with it the ability to cope with difficult situations. Under these circum-stances, we are easy prey for depression. Our defenses and our will to resist are weakened by the loss of confidence. We become pushovers.

Then, after we yield to depression we feel lost and helpless, unable to escape the oppressor. The suffering and the helplessness virtually wipe out whatever confidence is left in us. But, confidence is exactly what we need to fight depression. We cannot possibly even start to fight, let alone actually overcome depression, without a significant amount of trust in our ability to do so. Therefore, being able to put up an effective fight depends on our ability to regain our confidence and self-esteem in spite of the changes in our lives and in spite of depression.

Loss of confidence is self-inflicted, the product of a thought process just like everything else related to depression. This thought process is often triggered by actual events beyond our control, yet the loss of confidence as a result of these events is only a creation of our minds. Therefore, it is within our power to restrain this process and then to reverse it.

The way I see it, confidence in our own ability to do and achieve things is a function of how we perceive what we do, what we have achieved and what we are capable of doing. Things we believe we do well make us believe that we are capable of doing the same things and more, now or in the future. Achievements we are satisfied with boost our self-esteem and make us sure that we are capable of bigger and better achievements. On the other hand, failures and things we think that we are not good at make us feel insecure and doubtful.

I can come up with a list of at least twenty confidence-building things in my life at the snap of my finger, and so can you and everybody else. The items on each of our lists would be of various sizes. The big ones may be things like success in business, a solid career, athletic ability, a satisfying family life, a good social life, intellectual achievements or a talent for music. The small ones are mainly things that we have done and feel good about, like playing a good game of golf, earning compliments from the boss for a task well done, buying something at a good price or losing some weight.

Confidence, however, is not just a subjective evaluation of the separate items on our lists of confidence-building things, nor is it confined to those items. It is a feature of our character that affects everything that we do and shapes our viewpoint on life in general and on ourselves in particular. A high level of confidence not only makes us believe that we are capable of doing things, it actually makes us able to do them, while a low level of confidence makes us afraid even to try. This feature of character, this attitude, is made up of the contributions from all the big and small confidence-building things in our lives, like a structure made up of many building blocks. The more building blocks a person has and the bigger they are, the higher is the structure of his or her confidence.

Unfortunately, the building blocks of our confidence are neither rigid nor permanent. Many are temporary. For example, I may feel great about wining that game of tennis yesterday, which raises my confidence, but this effect will decay quickly and even be forgotten in a few days unless I win again, or if, heaven forbid, I lose. Most blocks, even the big ones, are pliable, expanding or shrinking according to events and circumstances. For example, success in one's career is clearly a big confidence-building block, but a single small failure can make it shrink dramatically, just as any success can make it expand.

So, the structure that is our confidence is not as solid and as steady as it may seem. It needs constant nourishment and replenishment even to stay as it is. Its size and shape fluctuates all the time, as building blocks expand or shrink, as new blocks are added and old ones removed according to what we do and what happens in our lives.

Midlife changes can erode or remove some of the building blocks of our confidence and it is enough to lose only a few of the fundamental blocks for the entire structure to cave in.

The changes are fairly common and we all tend to experience them in similar ways. We all go through menopause and feel the changes in our bodies and in our physical abilities that it brings. All of us have to cope with children growing up and going on their own ways, and many of us feel the progress in our careers grinding to a halt. For all of us, the relevant confidence building blocks are damaged. The differences among us are in how fundamental each such building block is to the entire structure of our confidence and in how much damage the structure can endure without collapsing. These differences stem from the differences in our character and in our way of life. For example, if sports and physical activity are not a main part of a woman's life, she may go through menopause hardly affected by the changes it causes in her body, while to someone like me these changes can bring a significant loss of confidence. Or, the confidence of a woman whose career is a central aspect of her life will suffer much more when that career becomes static than the confidence of someone who is perfectly happy with her career as it is and does not expect it to go anywhere.

For me, midlife changes shattered two main building blocks: responsibility for my children and control of my body.

Taking care of my children and being involved in every aspect of their lives was of paramount importance to me. When my oldest daughter left home for long backpacking trips abroad and then to live with her boyfriend, and when my son left home to go to the Army, something in me broke down. My children suddenly were out of my reach and out of my responsibility; they either did not need me as much as before or, if they did, there was not much I could do about it. A major component of my life shrunk to a fraction of what it had been, leaving a big void that I could not fill.

Menopause appeared hand in hand with a substantial decline in the athletic ability that I had taken for granted all my life. My body would no longer let me do the things I had been able to do so well just a short while earlier, no matter how hard I worked at it. Since so much of my life had revolved around sports and physical activities, being good at those things gave me a sense of self assurance, a kind of "I can do anything" attitude. When menopause reduced my athletic proficiency it also shattered that attitude and diminished my trust in myself in all things, not just where sports and athletics were involved.

These changes, which were spread over a couple of years, were probably not the only reason for my falling into depression, but they did give me a hard push towards it. Before those changes I was actively fulfilling what I perceived as my main purposes in life, namely taking care of my children and enjoying every moment of my life by doing the things I liked best. I had all the confidence in the world and was in full control of my life, with every aspect of it in place and working as smoothly as a perfectly tuned machine. A couple of years later, however, I had a big empty cavity where one of the main pillars of my life had been. And, on top of that, my tennis was in shambles. The importance I attach to tennis in this context is not as exaggerated as it may seem. What did most of the damage was not the inability to play as well as before but the loss of confidence that came with it. Just as being good at tennis had boosted my self-esteem and given me confidence overall, not just on the tennis court, so did the loss of that ability ruin my confidence in general. A big building block had turned to dust, leaving the entire structure in danger.

Each of us has her own fundamental blocks that can cause the collapse of the entire structure if they break down. Of course it would be best to avoid the breakdown altogether, but in most cases this is impossible because the causes are unavoidable. We cannot avoid menopause or prevent our children from growing up. We cannot stop the clock to prevent natural processes in our bodies, in our families or in our careers from running their course. It is a fact of life that fundamental building blocks will break down and that the structure of our confidence will be damaged. Some people are strong enough or lucky enough to be entirely impervious to all this. Most people manage to come through with only minor damage but for some, like me, the damage is quite substantial. What do we do then? We rebuild.

First, we must do damage assessment. What is it exactly that has been destroyed and what needs to be rebuilt? Although our loss of confidence makes us feel that everything is in ruins, that is simply not true. Of the many things that together make up what we think of as our lives, only a few are destroyed. All the others are either partially damaged or intact. What is destroyed and needs to be rebuilt is our confidence. Using the building block metaphor once more, very few blocks are actually destroyed; all the others are lying around where they fell when the structure collapsed. We just need to pick them up and rebuild the structure of our confidence.

Both the building of confidence and the loss of it are the products of similar processes. Our minds constantly evaluate our abilities and our achievements and then combine the results into a sort of a balance sheet. Things that get high marks in the evaluation build up our confidence and those that get low marks degrade it. Any evaluation is essentially a comparison against a scale. If I say that something is big, that is an evaluation that has no meaning unless I say big compared to what. An object can be big on one scale, say compared to a shoe and small on another scale, compared to a house, for instance. It is possible to tell whether something we have done is an achievement to be proud of or a failure, whether it should increase our confidence or decrease it, only if there is a scale to compare it with. The scale that the mind uses in this evaluation determines the outcome of the evaluation just as much as the issue that is being evaluated. The same achievement can boost our confidence when evaluated on one scale or make it plummet if another scale is used.

I believe that the mind measures achievements and abilities against scales that it builds separately for each aspect of our lives. For example, my mind has one scale for evaluating my tennis achievements, another scale for evaluating my performance at work, yet another for my evaluation of business matters and so on. Each scale is based on my perception of previous achievements in the respective area and on my perception of how these achievements compare with those of other people that I am in direct contact with. For example, I evaluate my tennis achievements against a scale based on my past performance and how it compares with other members of my club. My scores on this scale are sometimes high and sometimes low, with lots of so-so in between. But imagine how badly I would score on a scale based on the abilities of Wimbledon competitors.

When I feel that a change in my life ruins my abilities in some area, that simply means that my current performance scores very low grades on the scale that my mind uses for evaluation in that area. The same performance would have scored higher grades had my mind used another scale. Given that midlife changes and most of their consequences are beyond our control, the solution is to change the scales of evaluation when necessary. In other words, adjust our expectations rather than try to live up to standards that for the time being we cannot reach.

For example, I felt that the physical effects of menopause ruined my athletic ability and my tennis performance. What really happened was that my abilities, degraded by menopause, scored very low on my scale for things athletic, which was based on my previous abilities. But menopause did not destroy my abilities as completely as I felt it did. In fact, I could still play tennis, ride bicycles, run and swim, although not as well as before. But this deterioration, measured on that particular scale, scored so low that it made me lose all confidence in my ability. It was this loss of confidence, not the actual deterioration that made me throw in the towel and stop playing tennis. What I should have done, had I recognized what was happening, was to modify my scale of reference by reducing my expectations. In practical terms, that means I should have simply played with weaker partners, not the ones at my previous level.

What builds up or destroys our confidence is the score, not the actual achievement. And, the score depends on the scale. An achievement that scores high on a modest scale of reference contributes to our self-esteem and confidence just as much as a greater achievement that gets the same score on a more demanding scale. So, we should not let changes in our life and the decline that they may cause in some aspects of it destroy our confidence. If we adjust our scale of reference to the new situation, what appears to be a confidence-wrecking disappointment can become the beginning of a confidence-building accomplishment.

How does one adjust her scales of reference?

The first step is awareness. We are dealing here with a process of causes and effects tied together like the links of a chain. Each link is the product of the one that precedes it and the cause of the one that follows. The first link in the chain is the result of actual circumstances, such as menopause and children growing up, which change our life and our bodies. The next link is a decline in our capabilities and achievements in some areas, combined with a loss of some of the main focal points of our lives. This leads to the next link, which is the loss of confidence. The last link in the chain is part of depression: sensations of being worthless, loss of the ability and the will to do many things in life that we used to do before, a dominant sensation of anxiety and of feeling bad, both mentally and physically.

It is this last link that we are mainly aware of; the others are circumstantial as far as our consciousness is concerned. To turn the process around we first must become aware of all the links in the chain and understand the cause and effect mechanisms by which it works.

Then we need to look carefully at the things each of us feels she can no longer do because of depression. The statement "I cannot do this anymre" is essentially an evaluation against a scale of reference. In reality, that statement means: "I cannot do this as well as before or as much as before". Things are not either black or white. They are always some shade of gray, but we make them seem black by comparing them against an inappropriate scale of reference. When I say that I cannot work, the term "work" has a very definite meaning in my mind. It means the job I had before, the amount of hours I used to spend there every day, the organization, the responsibilities, the boss, the colleagues, the commute, even the coffee machine. Compared to that picture in my mind, it may be true that "I cannot work" but does that mean that I can do no work at all, under any different interpretation of the term "work?" Most probably not, but by using a scale of reference that is no longer adequate, my mind sets in motion the process I have just described. It is this process that makes me lose confidence in my ability to work and eventually makes me believe that I am totally unable to work.

The same is true for most things a person suffering from depression believes he or she cannot do. When you feel "I cannot do this" it means you cannot do what your mind holds "this" to be. In other words, your mind is using the wrong scale of reference. It may be a fact that you are able to do less of whatever "this" happens to be than you could do before, but less is not necessarily equal to zero. There is always something, no matter how small, that you can do. Do it, and then adjust the scale of reference so that this something becomes your yardstick. That may sound fuzzy but actually it is quite simple: Do whatever you can and measure yourself against what you can do.

In the darkest periods of depression I was unable to do even the most simple and ordinary things, such as preparing dinner for my family or reading a book. So, instead of preparing dinner I decided that I would only make the salad, nothing more. The salad became my new yardstick and when, after a while, I managed to do a little more, such as salad and coffee, or a simple dish, it gave me a sense of satisfaction and with that a small bit of confidence. When I was unable to keep my mind in one place long enough to read, I decided to read just one page and then put the book down. At first I used to stare at that page or read the words several times before actually making sense of what they meant. Then it started to work, and when I moved up to reading two or three pages it felt good and gave me the confidence to move up to more.

The key word in this entire issue is to do. When you feel that you cannot do something, reduce the scope of whatever that something is until it becomes small and simple enough to handle or break it down into small tasks that can be done one at a time. Then go ahead and do it. Do it again and again until you can do a little more. Throw away your old scale of reference and use what you can actually do as the new scale. Any small progress on the new scale will add a little bit to your confidence and make you able to do a little more. This is very similar to that chain process, only in reverse. On the new scale of reference, whatever you can do becomes a small achievement that builds up your confidence and your ability to do a little more and then a little more again and again. It does not matter how low the starting point is; it may be just a salad or a single page. The only thing that matters is to do and to keep the process of confidence buildup in motion.

Of course, you need motivation to get that process started. It is easier to give up altogether, especially since you often may feel that giving up is fully justified under the circumstances. Thoughts like, "Let's face it, I cannot do this, so what is the use?" are always ready to pop up in our minds. Motivation to do things and actually doing them are, in this case, like the chicken and the egg. Doing brings confidence, which creates motivation to do more. The reverse is also true, without doing, there is no confidence and therefore no motivation. So forget about motivation, just do it and motivation will follow.

You will discover that similarly to how it works in the destructive process, building up of confidence is not confined by rigid boundaries. An increased level of confidence in one area projects confidence on other areas and creates the motivation to do and to rebuild them as well. Any confidence-building progress in one area is an incentive to do and achieve a little more in other areas. Confidence is a cumulative attitude that is built up with any single specific success but applies to life in general. Once this attitude starts to build up it will affect every aspect of your life and soon you will discover that you are capable of doing more things in more areas with less effort.

Once under way, the process of reconstruction will spread to all areas of your life and rebuild the general structure of your confidence. It will probably be a different structure than the one you had before, but it can be just as high or even higher. The new structure will be designed for your current life, not for what it used to be years before, with properly adjusted scales of reference and a general attitude of confidence oriented towards the future, not looking back over your shoulder into the past. When that happens, the one thing you can look at over your shoulder will be depression. It will become a thing of the past.

REBUILD CONFIDENCE
SUMMARY

- Regaining confidence is essential for getting rid of depression.

- Loss of confidence is a self-inflicted thought process. It is within your power to reverse this process.

- Confidence is built up or lost by comparison to scales of reference. Adjust your scales of reference to the current conditions.

- Start rebuilding from the ground up. Do everything that you did before but within your current abilities, do less of everything but do not give anything up. Measure yourself against what you can do now, not against what you could do before.

- Forget the "I cannot do this anymore" nonsense. Just keep doing. Doing brings confidence and motivation to do more.

Tactic #8
Practice Mental Techniques

All measures we can take against depression must affect our mind in one way or another because the mind is what depression is all about. That is the objective of every one of the methods and measures I have described above, which approach the mind from different directions and on different routes. Mental techniques are a family of measures that take a more direct route than the others.

These techniques are mental in the sense that they work directly on the mind, not because they are applied mentally, although many of them are. Some mental techniques are applied physically and some through a combination of physical and mental activities.

These techniques are the mental equivalent of physical exercises and physical therapy combined. They work on the mind like their physical counterparts work on the body, making it stronger, more resilient and more disciplined. In my experience, these techniques are very helpful in the struggle against depression and even more effective after victory. Like in most victories, military, political or any other type, the enemy does not disappear in a puff of smoke. It is still there, constantly trying to come back at you. Victory over depression is achieved when you reach a point where you are fully in control and able to repel any attempt it makes to take over again. This is where the mental techniques become a very effective weapon.

It is not the goal of this chapter to teach mental techniques. My objective is to impress upon you the understanding that mental techniques work very effectively and are well worth the effort required to acquire and apply them. To do so, I can only use my experience, gained in almost ten years of learning and practicing these techniques, and describe which techniques I use and how I use them. What I practice is tailored for me, the product of experimentation with many techniques in a process of trial and elimination. This should serve mainly as an illustration, not as a guide. What works best for me does not necessarily have to be the best for you. Every person has his or her specific set of "best" mental techniques. All you have to do is to find yours.

I use three mental techniques. Why three? Because out of the dozen or so that I have tried, these three work for me and because one is not enough. No matter how well a technique works for you, at times it will simply not deliver, or you will not be able to apply it properly. At such times, it is better to switch to something else and you should have that something else ready at hand. There is also an upper limit. Mental techniques need practice just as much, or maybe more than, physical exercise. If you practice too many techniques, then by necessity you will practice less of each. So, two to five is about the right range. In my case, it happens to be three.

The three techniques I use are: Relaxation, Autosuggestion and Guided Imagery.

Relaxation

I use this technique to remove tension from my body and relieve the physical sensations of pressure in my head and tightness in the back of my neck. It is very helpful by itself or as a preliminary stage from which I proceed to other techniques.

What I discovered to be most important for relaxation to work is to just let it happen. If I do the routine without thinking about relaxation, without expecting it and without making any conscious effort to make it happen, my body responds and relaxes.

Relaxation works best in a quiet place where I can be alone and undisturbed for twenty or thirty minute, although now, with experience, I can do it almost anywhere and at any time.

To start, I recline in a comfortable position and take a deep breath through my nose, trying to inhale as much air as I can. I hold my breath to the count of five and then exhale slowly through my mouth, again to the count of five. I repeat this process for several minutes, trying to imagine that energy flows into my body when I inhale and tension flows out when I exhale.

Then I focus my attention on one foot and feel the tension leaving it; sometimes I even feel my foot getting warmer as it relaxes. Then I move my attention to the other foot and relax it as well. I move slowly up my body, from foot to calf, from calf to thigh and so on, focusing on every part and relaxing it before moving to the next. With every new step, I feel the already relaxed parts of my body getting more and more relaxed until my entire body sinks into a state of deep relaxation. I can make this state even deeper by imagining that I am in a calm and beautiful place. A beach at sunset is my favorite.

Once I am fully relaxed I use Autosuggestion or Guided Imagery, or just lie down and enjoy.

This relaxation routine is just one of many variations on the same theme. Some variations use calm music, others use a narrator with a deep authoritative voice that guides the listener step by step. There are many guidebooks and courses that teach relaxation. All variations and all ways to learn the technique are fine because they all lead to the same goal. It is just a matter of finding the version that works best for you.

Autosuggestion

Autosuggestion is a deceptively simple technique that works surprisingly well. It comes complete with a deep theory about the conscious and subconscious minds. Generally, I do not get into the psychological theories of the mental techniques I practice, just as I do not get into the theory of Hydrodynamics when I swim. The only thing that matters to me is whether it works, not how or why it works. But in this case the theory is part of the practice, so here it is in a nutshell.

According to the father of this theory, a French psychotherapist named Emile Coue, we have a conscious mind and a subconscious mind. The latter determines what we do and what we feel no less than the conscious mind, although we are usually not directly aware of it. When there is a contradiction between the two, when our reasoning conscious mind will have us do one thing and the subconscious mind wants us to do another, the subconscious will usually prevail. To the subconscious mind, there is no distinction between what is real and what is not. In other words, to the subconscious mind everything it accepts is real as far as it is concerned. The main idea is to implant a notion, or a suggestion in Coue's terminology, into the subconscious mind. But the subconscious mind will not accept just anything. It will not accept notions that are not feasible or notions that somehow go against the grain of its internal logic. Once it accepts a notion, the subconscious mind will treat it as reality and enforce it upon our feelings and behavior just as it enforces any instinct, without objective reasons or even in spite of such reasons. I think of this as a way to get at the mind through a back door.

Here is how I do it. First, I select a suggestion, which must be something I want to achieve and is within my capability to achieve. The suggestion should be phrased in a positive statement. For example, if the goal is to get rid of the sensation of pressure in my head, the suggestion can be: "The pressure is getting lower and lower." To phrase the same suggestion in a negative statement such as "There is no pressure" would not work. Then, usually in a state of relaxation, I repeat that phrase slowly and monotonously twenty times like a mantra in meditation. I do this without really thinking about the meaning of the words and without trying to enforce the suggestion.

That is all, and it works. Somehow the suggestion becomes a reality. And, by using the same suggestions regularly, it becomes easier to make them work as time goes by. Monsieur Coue would say that the repetition implants the suggestion deeper and deeper into my subconscious mind. Be that as it may, Autosuggestion is easy and works almost every time, and that is all that really counts.

Guided Imagery

The way I see it, Guided Imagery is very similar to Autosuggestion in that it implants notions into the subconscious mind, which accepts them as reality. The difference is in the language. Autosuggestion uses words, while Guided Imagery "talks" to the subconscious mind in images, which are more akin to its "natural language." Supposedly, the subconscious mind handles information in the form that the senses perceive it, as images and sounds, not as words and ideas. Images are, therefore, a more direct means of communicating with the subconscious and implanting in it the desired notion.

I use Guided Imagery when in a relaxed state and also whenever I feel anxiety and pressure beginning to build up. I often practice it while swimming or running.

The technique is to visualize, to create an imaginary visual picture, like a very short video clip, of what I want to happen. The picture does not have to be realistic; it can be quite metaphoric because, after all, I am "talking" to the part of my mind that deals with imagination and dreams, not to the part that deals with logic.

Here are some examples. When I feel that my head becomes very heavy I visualize it as being a balloon, very light and floating in the air. When I feel pressure in my head, I visualize that I am wearing a very tight and rigid helmet; then I visualize the helmet breaking up into small pieces that fall off in all directions. When I use Guided Imagery while swimming, I visualize a flood of pure water flowing through my body, not around it, carrying away the tensions.

The best part about Guided Imagery is that it works almost instantly. When I use it to relieve tensions and pressure, it makes them disappear right away and leaves me feeling calm and free from anxiety. The very knowledge that I possess this power to get rid of the bad feelings at will is in itself very reassuring. Even the worst monster is not frightening if you can make it vanish with a snap of your finger.

It is very easy to learn and to practice mental techniques and, when you find the ones that work for you, they actually work very well. You can learn these techniques the usual ways: books, courses and practice. In my view there are two keys to success: approach them with an open mind and focus on the practical aspects.

Many of the mental techniques are quite obscure, or at least appear so to a novice. Some go against the grain of our logic and way of thinking. That should be understandable because, in essence, they aim for the non-logical parts of our minds. It is quite natural for a rational, thinking person to be incredulous, even resentful of these techniques and to dismiss them as mere nonsense. However, this approach will get you nowhere. I recommend that you employ an "I will try anything once" approach. Leave rational prejudices aside and just give it a chance. A little curiosity about new things might also help. And, when you try a new technique do it without hesitations or reservations. Then, if it works, fine. If it does not work, at least you know that you have given it a fair chance and that it is truly not the right technique for you.

Every technique comes complete with a theory of operation. Some theories are essentially scientific and quite fascinating to read and learn. Other theories may be esoteric or even implausible. Most books and a good part of the courses that teach this or that technique tend to present it through the theory, trying to convince you of its truth before teaching you how to practice it. There is absolutely nothing wrong with this approach, but in my opinion it is better to focus on the practical part. First, learn what to do and how to practice the technique, giving it full credit for being based on a sound and true theory. If it does not work, you will discard it anyway. If it does work and you decide to adopt it, this may be the time to go back and learn about the theory behind it if you are so inclined.

The main point is to try. At least some of the many available techniques can certainly help you very much. It is just a matter of trying and choosing. Once you find those techniques that are right for you, their practice will become a habit. They also will become a priceless means to overcome depression and improve the quality of your life in general.

MENTAL TECHNIQUES
SUMMARY

- Mental techniques are the mental equivalent of physical exercises and physical therapy combined. They make the mind stronger, more resilient and more disciplined.

- It is very easy to learn mental techniques through books, courses and practice, and they actually work very well.

- Approach each technique with an open mind and focus on the practical aspects, not the theories. First, learn what to do and find out if it works. If it does, you can learn more about the theory behind it.

- Experiment with many techniques to find those that work for you.

Tactic #9
Daily Workout

What should a person who is physically out of shape do to get into shape? The answer is obvious: exercise. That person should exercise not only when she gets out of breath after climbing one flight of stairs and then do nothing until she has to climb some stairs again. She has to exercise regularly and systematically to build up her physical fitness. And when she does, no flight of stairs will get her out of breath although she does nothing in particular to prepare for that specific situation.

Depression is like being out of shape mentally. We need to exercise to regain our mental fitness and get back into shape, and then we need to exercise to stay in shape. Like our friend who is out of breath, we must exercise regularly and methodically, every single day, not just when we feel bad. We need to set up a daily routine of mental workouts to build up and maintain our mental fitness.

The mental workout should typically consist of doing sets of mental techniques like one does sets on the exercise machines in the gym. I work out every morning just after I get up and every evening. Each workout consists of relaxation followed by sessions of Autosuggestion and Guided Imagery. I use the same suggestion phrases and the same images every time. A typical workout lasts twenty to thirty minutes and I do it every day, not just when I feel bad.

Every woman should build her own set of mental exercises from the mental techniques that work for her and do that set every day, preferably more than once a day. As with physical exercises, practice makes perfect. After doing the daily workout for some time it becomes both easier and more effective than when you are starting out. But, unlike the physical equivalent, there is no need to move up to a higher level of difficulty as you would add weights on the machines in the gym. It is quite sufficient, in fact probably even better, to stick to the same set of exercises. The main thing is just to do them every day.

Your daily workout should not consist entirely of mental exercise. Physical exercise is just as important to the fitness of our minds as it is to the fitness of our bodies and should, therefore, be part of your daily routine.

Without getting into a discussion of Body-Mind relationship, although it is truly a fascinating issue, let me point out some practical aspects in the context of depression.

Being physically fit gives us a sense of confidence and self-esteem. It is something that we are good at and that makes a significant contribution to our confidence. This boost to our confidence is not limited to sports and fitness alone; it extends into all other areas of our life and has a very positive effect on everything that we do. Being fit makes us feel good and look good, which works wonders in building confidence.

All the tactics you will employ to overcome depression require self-discipline, stamina and perseverance. These characteristics must be acquired deliberately and nurtured constantly, they do not "just happen" to be part of one's personality. There is nothing like regular physical exercise to embed self-discipline in our personality, to build up our stamina, both physical and mental and to make them inherent features of our character.

Regular physical exercise affects depression directly. A good session of exercise, followed by a nice hot shower invariably purges stress out of our minds and tension out of our bodies, which is just another way of saying that it drives depression out of our mind, at least for awhile.

So, in many senses physical exercises are also very important mental exercises and should be an indispensable part of your daily workout.

DAILY WORKOUT
SUMMARY

- You need mental exercise to regain your mental fitness, to get back into shape and to stay in shape.

- You must exercise regularly and methodically, every single day.

- Set up a daily routine of mental workouts that consists of doing sets of mental techniques like one does sets on the exercise machines in the gym.

- Physical exercise is just as important to the fitness of your mind as it is to the fitness of your body and should, therefore, be part of your daily routine.

Tactic #10
Prepare for Emergency

In addition to the workouts done on a regular basis, we need some special tools to be used in cases of emergency, when depression threatens to gain the upper hand in spite of everything we do. Such situations may emerge for any number of reasons or for no reason at all. When they do, we should be prepared.

The signs of depression are very familiar to those of us who have experienced them so many times before. Just feeling those signs should be like an alarm on a warship calling the crew to battle stations. There is no need to wait for anything and no room for delay or hesitation. We should take action immediately, and the sooner we do the easier it will be to drive out the aggressor. If we remain passive, if we just sit and wait, the situation will get worse fast and will be so much more difficult to get out of.

What should one do when the alarm sounds? Our metaphoric ship is drifting towards depression and we should take control of the helm and steer the ship in another direction. Our mind is drifting towards the bad thoughts that bring stress and anxiety. We must turn it around to the opposite direction, drive out the bad thoughts and replace them with good ones.

Sounds simplistic? Maybe, but it works, and not only for depression.

Take anger, for example. Every person has a hate-list of things that make him or her angry: the boss, some political issue, taxes, crime, the mother in law, whatever. If you think for a minute or two about the thing that is at the top of your hate-list, whatever it may be, you will most probably feel angry. This will cause you to think more and harder about that hateful thing and the anger will build up. Some people can think themselves into a fit of rage without any external stimulus, merely because the object of their anger happens to cross their mind. Now, when you feel the anger, if you switch your thoughts to something that gives you pleasure, such as your next vacation, the anger will disappear immediately.

When my mind is filled with anxiety and I feel the familiar pressures, I make a deliberate effort to switch my thoughts to something good and enjoyable. There are good things to think about at any time. Right now I might think of the great new job that my son got recently or about my oldest daughter and my first grandson who will come to visit us next month. Or I might think about the tennis tournament I won last week or the Triathlon this weekend. On second thought, scratch the Triathlon; it will qualify as a good thought after it is over. Thinking about such things breaks the cycle of stress, anxiety and more stress. The good thought practically cleanses the mind of the bad and makes me feel better.

The key is to be able to make the switch. When the bad thoughts have a grip on your mind, they may resist being replaced by other thoughts. When you try to switch the mind to good thoughts, it will simply drift back to the bad ones. You may also have difficulty in finding something good to think about right at that moment. It is helpful to always have one or two good thoughts ready at any time, so that when you try to switch there will be no need to search for something to switch to. As may be obvious from these examples, I prefer to use actual and current events as themes for good thoughts. That, of course, is individual, but there may be a reason why such themes work better. Unlike memories of things long gone or thoughts about abstract or distant issues, like peace on earth or winning a jackpot in Vegas, current and concrete themes invoke emotions. For example, I can feel the joy of winning the final match last weekend and the excitement when thinking about my grandson's visit next month. These emotions help the good thoughts take over and drive the bad ones out.

When just coming up with a theme for a good thought is not enough to drive out the bad thoughts, additional measures can help make the switch. The most effective way is to get up and do something, like taking a walk, listening to my favorite music, playing the piano, anything that will take my mind off the bad feelings and clear the way for good thoughts to replace the bad.

The main thing is not to get stuck in a static position, physically or mentally, when the bad feelings of depression show up. To remain passive at such times is to give depression free rein to amplify the anxiety that causes the bad feeling and through it to intensify them, only to amplify anxiety some more, and so on. It is essential to break this cycle and reverse its course. This can be done mentally, by turning attention away from the bad thoughts and replacing them with good ones. It can be done physically, by getting up and doing something different, preferably also enjoyable, just to make a change. And, it can be done by a combination of both.

The signs of depression should set off an alarm, complete with a loud siren and flashing red lights. At the sound of this alarm, you should jump into action and turn your mind in the direction opposite from the one it was heading to. But sometimes even that is not enough.

Emergency situations come in various levels of severity. A minor emergency can be the result of increased stress and can be easily chased away by thinking about something good. At the other end of the scale are the really severe emergency situations, when the pull of depression is so strong that it drags you into its depths no matter what you try to do to hold on.

Drastic situations call for drastic measures. The methods are the same but they should be applied with maximum intensity.

The first thing I do when I find myself in a severe emergency is to make a total commitment not to give in, no matter what. I have been at the bottom of the pit of depression and I have fought my way out. Nothing will ever drag me back down. Then I try to turn my mind away, in the opposite direction from where depression is pulling it, with every bit of mental strength that I have. I drop everything I am doing or am supposed to do and go do something that will get me back in control. For instance, I go to the gym and work out to exhaustion or swim in the pool as fast and as long as I can. The idea is not just to think about things that make me feel good but to actually do them at the highest level of intensity and to the exclusion of everything else.

I cannot recommend to you specific things to do in cases of severe emergency. All I can say is this: Severe emergencies will happen and you must be ready for them. First, make a total, irrevocable commitment to hold on and never give in to depression again. Then, do whatever works best for you, at the highest intensity possible. Drop everything else you are doing and concentrate all your energy, all your physical and mental strength on getting out. Take a day off from everything and go do the thing you enjoy most, forgetting about anything else. Devise your own emergency measures and use them vigorously. Just fight back and fight hard.

PREPARE FOR EMERGENCY
SUMMARY

- You need special tools to be used in cases of emergency when depression threatens to gain the upper hand.

- The familiar signs of depression should be like an alarm calling to battle stations. Take action immediately and make a U-turn. Drive your mind in the opposite direction from where it was heading.

- Make the U-turn mentally. Turn attention away from the bad thoughts and replace them with good thoughts that will cleanse the mind and make you feel better.

- Make the U-turn physically. Get up and do something different, preferably also enjoyable, just to make a change.

- In severe emergency situations, make a total commitment to hold on and never give in to depression again, then apply the same methods with maximum intensity.

When it all Comes Together

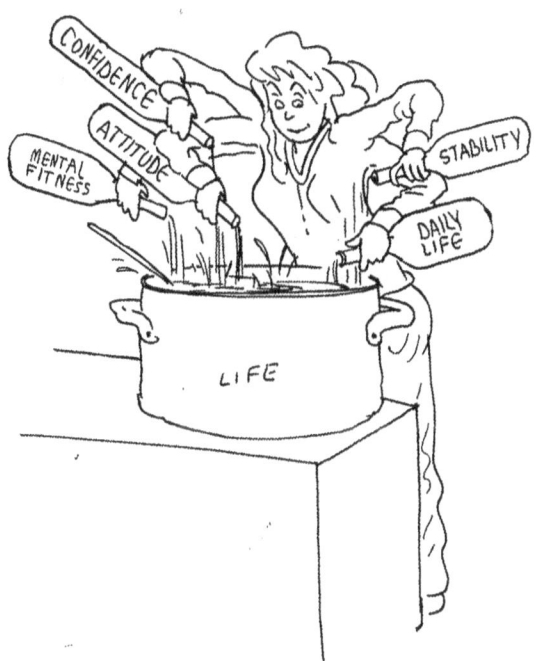

The preceding chapters present courses of action. The theme is: do this and do that. Now let us consider what will happen when you do the things that those chapters recommend.

In fighting depression you move forward in life, not backward. The fight will not take you back to where you had been before depression started. Your life will not be exactly the same as it was then and, more significantly, you will not be exactly the same person. Your life will not be a "New Life" either, nor will you become a "New Person." To use those terms in this context would be a gross exaggeration. The tactics recommended in the previous chapters will bring about adaptations of life and personality rather than a transformation. Several such adaptations will occur, some subtle, others more obvious. Each of them, although it may contribute significantly to the fight, will not in itself be enough to win it. When they all come together, the combined result will be victory over depression.

If you look at the diagram below, you will certainly recognize the pattern of its left part. Each block corresponds to a chapter in the book and the pattern has been building up gradually with the addition of each chapter. These blocks actually represent all the tactics that I have been urging you to employ. The blocks on the right are the result of applying all those tactics as recommended. These are the adaptations of life and personality that together will bring you victory. Let us consider them one by one.

The Road Map to Victory

Daily Life

By daily life I mean your daily routine, everything you do and how you do it. That includes work, social life, family life, hobbies, sports and everything else that depression has been trying to take away from you. Many of the tactics you use in your fight are aimed at getting all that back. From rebuilding confidence in your ability to do things, through restructuring daily routine to staying busy at all times and learning to take control of thought processes, everything leads to regaining the capacity to lead a full and active life.

Gradually, slowly at first and then at an ever accelerating pace, pieces of your daily life that have been lost to depression will come back and fit together again. Eventually, you will regain the ability to do everything that was part of your life before depression and your daily life will become as full and active as it was then. You will most probably discover that you have acquired an appetite for doing even more than before.

Yet this life will be adjusted to the new situation you live in.

There will be new habits and a re-organization of your time, stemming from the deliberate effort to keep busy, which by now will have become second nature, and from the daily exercise of mental workouts.

There will be some changes in the environment you live in due to the changes that your family and friends will have gone through in the course of your fight. What they learn about depression will not be erased. What they do to support you in your fight and the ordeal your family and you will have gone through together can only improve the relationships and strengthen the bonds within the family.

The struggle to return from depression-induced passivity to a fully active life will focus your priorities and make those things that are the most significant stand out. When it takes an effort to do things, one naturally learns to distinguish between what is important and what is not, then invests her efforts accordingly. On the other hand, when everything comes easily there is no incentive to prioritize and choose.

Therefore, there will be things in your previous life that you decide to give up and new things you adopt.

Having made such efforts to regain the ability to do things will also make you appreciate and enjoy what you do rather than taking everything for granted.

Attitude

Your fight against depression will affect the way you think about yourself, your life and the world you live in. The fight starts with a resolution to take control, built upon what I called in previous chapters an ideology, a firm and unquestioning belief in your ability to beat depression. I used strong words in those chapters to inspire and persuade you to make the crucial decision to fight. I must admit to a certain level of hand waving and slogan shouting in those statements. The truth is that the firm belief, the ideology, develops and grows during the fight itself, nourished by the very courses of action that follow the decision to take control. It is basically a chicken-and-egg situation that must be put in motion; hence, the strong statements that, I truly hope, by now have fully served their purpose.

Every course of action presented in the previous chapters enhances the belief in your ability to fight and win. Every step you take and any amount of progress you make along any of those courses of action proves that your decision to take control and fight was the right decision and therefore also strengthens your belief in the ideology that your fight is based on.

This belief, once fully acquired, becomes your attitude toward life and an integral part of your personality. This attitude and this ideology, now firmly based on actual achievements and not just on inspiring words, will propel you towards victory and will make you a better and stronger person long after victory is achieved.

Confidence

Rebuilding confidence is the goal of one of the tactics, yet confidence will not come only from that. It will also come from your ability to beat the bad thoughts of depression and drive them out of your mind, from the newly acquired skills in use of mental techniques, from the knowledge that you can count on the support of your family and that your doctor, the right doctor, is always there when needed. Anything that works in any course of action, every little progress and every achievement, helps build up your confidence and makes it easier to do more and achieve more.

Mental Fitness

Mental fitness is very similar to physical fitness. Being mentally fit means that your mind has the strength, the training and the resilience to cope with difficulties that would overpower a weaker mind. It means that your mind has the power and the stamina to exert efforts that would leave an unfit mind gasping for breath.

Fitness comes from training. With mental fitness, that means the constant exercise of mental techniques. Fitness also comes from the application of mental power in the other courses of action, just as physical work builds up muscles. The constant mental efforts you make to control bad thoughts, the mental exertion required to rebuild your confidence and the mental struggle with depression to regain control of your life will all build up your mental muscle.

Stability

Several of the tactics will help you smooth out the bumpy ups and downs, or should I say shallow downs and deep downs, of depression. The support from family and friends, the advice and constant support of your doctor, taking medications as needed and the use of mental techniques, the so-called emergency toolkit whenever depression tries to pull you down, all these provide stability. They provide a steady platform to stand on, a sure footing from which to wage your fight.

A rebuilt daily life, a strong can-do attitude, confidence, mental fitness and stability are the elements that victory is made of. Each tactic contributes to several or all of the elements and each element is based on several tactics. No single tactic and no single element can beat depression. When you apply all tactics concurrently, all the elements come together and victory is yours.

Life After Victory

Life is what this book is all about, not depression. It is about the fight to rebuild Life after it has been damaged or ruined by depression. The fight is for Life, not against depression. Beating depression is not the goal, only a means to achieve the goal. And the goal is Life.

By "Life" I mean everything that you do, everything that you have and especially what you enjoy having or doing. Life is family, work, sports, hobbies, friends, home, vacations, religion, politics and so on and on. Life is what you are and what you have put together from early childhood as best you can, given your character, talents, luck, education and the countless other things that make Life what it is.

When depression comes and destroys all that, it takes Life away from you.

Victory comes when you are again able to live Life as fully as before and to enjoy it at least as much. That is the one and only criterion for victory, the single objective to fight for. Anything less than that is an unsatisfactory compromise. The long and arduous journey that began with the decision to take control and fight for your Life cannot stop short of the ultimate goal.

Unfortunately, the fight is not over when you do reach the goal. Victory, as sweet as it may be, is not absolute, not even final. Victories seldom are, as history proves again and again. After victory you have your Life back to live and enjoy, but the enemy is still there. You can subdue it, you can keep it at bay and you can drive it back into the dark hole where it came from, but you cannot drive it completely out of your mind. Depression will try to take advantage of any opportunity to harass you. A stressful situation or a setback in any aspect of your life, and sometimes no apparent reason at all, may bring back the familiar sensations of depression. So the fight for Life must go on; only this time the goal is to keep Life, not to regain it.

Dealing with depression after victory is similar to the initial fight in that the enemy is the same and the weapons are also the same, but in every other respect it is entirely a new ballgame. First, because now the roles are reversed, you are in control and depression is the one fighting for survival. And, most important, you are not the same person that allowed depression to take over her Life. Having fought and won, you are now equipped with powers and skills that make you an awesome anti-depression combatant.

All that you have done to overcome depression is now a part of you. All your learning and experience, the education of your family and friends, their learning and experience in fighting at your side, your built-up confidence, your attitude toward life, the lifestyle and habits you adapted to cope with depression, all these are always at your disposal. Also at your disposal are your mental techniques and emergency measures. And, in case of extreme need, so is medical help from a doctor you can trust without reservation. It is all integrated and working together smoothly, like a well-tuned machine, oiled with experience and fueled by your newly regained Life.

Like any real machine, this allegoric machine also needs care and maintenance. Left unattended, it may get out of tune and eventually grind to a halt. I strongly recommend that you continue to practice your daily workout regularly, including, of course, physical fitness exercises, to stay in top shape, both mentally and physically. By now this workout should be so embedded in your lifestyle and daily routine that there really is no need for my recommendation.

Beyond your workouts, the name of the game is vigilance and awareness. You should be alert to any signs of depression and to any situation that it may take advantage of. When you detect such signs, it is important to react promptly and vigorously, using the skills and methods at your disposal, to restrain depression right away. In doing so, your victory over depression becomes complete.

You are now free to live and enjoy Life.

Afterthoughts

After all is said and done there are still some disturbing thoughts gnawing at the back of my mind. It is all very well to put up a big fight, with a grand strategy and multiple tactics and score a great victory. But it would have been much better and wiser to avoid the entire war altogether.

I keep asking myself: Was it at all possible to stop the collapse into depression at the very beginning? Could I identify the problem when it was still in the making? Could I have done something to prevent it from growing into monstrous dimensions? Even with the wisdom of hindsight I cannot come up with a definite and positive answer to these questions, just a big maybe.

Suppose, just for the sake of argument, that I could know then what I know now. Suppose that by some miracle I could have read this book at the very beginning of my troubles. What would I have done? Or, rather, what should I have done? These are, of course, hypothetical questions and, as far as I am concerned, pure speculation. But they may be quite relevant questions for other people that are now at that early phase when they can still avoid their collapse into depression.

Suppose that some hypothetical person, whom I shall call Dalia B, is just now experiencing the first signs of menopause. Also suppose that by coincidence she happens to come across this book. What will she do? First of all, will she read it? Probably not. The title says: depression. Why should Dalia B read books about a predicament she does not have? After all, she does not have anything to do with depression, she just has menopause. But, suppose that out of sheer curiosity, or maybe because she likes the picture on the cover, or perhaps because a friend recommends it, she does read this book. What can she learn from it that is applicable to her present situation?

The first thing she can learn is that there is a direct path form where she is to the depths of depression and that, if she is careless and unaware, she may find herself walking down that path without even being aware of where she is going until it is too late. She probably feels already the physiological effects of that period in her life, manifested in any one or several of many ways: cramps, back aches, loss of physical fitness, whatever. She may also experience changes in her life that occur at about the same time: children leaving the house, career problems, etc. But she probably does not suspect that these may snowball into a major mental problem.

If by reading this book she becomes aware, at an early enough stage, of the possible linkage between the physiological phenomena she is experiencing and the mental problems that lie like traps in her way, if she learns how to bypass those traps without falling into them, then she may be able to win her war with depression before it has even started, and for that I will envy her tremendously.

So, now that Dalia B knows about the path from menopause to depression, what can she learn from this book that will keep her off that path? I believe that the first thing to learn is resilience. The biggest mistake she can make is to stand unbending and rigid in the face of the inevitable changes rather than adapt to them, bend a little if necessary and let them pass. No heroic efforts are required and no big sacrifices are involved. On the contrary, it is an obstinate ignorant, as I was at the time, who would make an effort to hold her ground without giving an inch and would end up making tremendous sacrifices to regain what she should not have lost in the first place. Dalia B can and should be smarter than that. Realizing that her life is undergoing a change she cannot fight, she should accept the changes and simply live with them. From where she is now this may look like a painful sacrifice. But if she understands that the alternative may well be to follow the route I took, which was tremendously more painful, I have no doubt that she will make the right decisions. I have no specific advice to give on exactly how to do that because I have not done it myself. I took the other route. So I must leave it to her common sense to find the way to live with her changed life and to adapt to whatever limitations, real or apparent, that life may imply. I can only hope that this book motivates her to find that way and that the tactics and methods presented here will point her in the right direction.

Now suppose, just to take this line of thought one step further, that my new friend Dalia B has somehow missed the opportunity to stay away from the traps of depression. Maybe she did not come across this book in time, or maybe she found it irrelevant and put it away. What then? Is she doomed to fall all the way down to the bottom before she starts to fight her way back out? Does she have to wait until she reaches a desperate situation before she takes control of her life and fights back? Definitely not. She should start fighting back the moment she feels the grip of depression and, the sooner she starts the easier and swifter will be her victory.

The ideology and tactics set forth in this book should be applied at the earliest stage possible. In the most fortunate case that Dalia B gets the message before she falls into the trap, she need not really apply them at all. Just the awareness of the danger and some general guidance she can derive from the tactics should be sufficient to keep her safe from depression. If she does fall into the trap then time is of the essence. She must take control and start the fight at the earliest possible moment. It is like sliding down a steep slope into an abyss. The sooner she starts to climb back up, the shorter and easier will be the climb. If she lets herself slide long and deep before she starts to climb back, the climb will be much longer and more difficult.

Now of course Dalia B is only a metaphor, although I am beginning to like her. She is here to serve a purpose. This entire book is about what I did. She is here to point out what I should have done. In the hope that you, the reader, are still at the early stages where the fight must really begin, her message to you, and mine, is: Please, please do not delay. TAKE CONTROL AND START FIGHTING RIGHT NOW.

0-595-28469-8

www.ingramcontent.com/pod-product-compliance
Lightning Source LLC
Chambersburg PA
CBHW061404280526
45784CB00001B/362